celebrate
GOOD TIMES!

celebrate
GOOD TIMES!

26 COMPLETE PARTIES for Church and Home

Elizabeth Whitney Crisci

JUDSON PRESS
PUBLISHERS SINCE 1824

V A L L E Y   F O R G E ,   P A

Celebrate Good Times!
26 Complete Parties for Church and Home

© 2005 by Judson Press, Valley Forge, PA 19482-0851
All rights reserved.

Judson Press has made every effort to trace the ownership of all quotes. In the event of a question arising from the use of a quote, we regret any error made and will be pleased to make the necessary correction in future printings and editions of this book.

Bible quotations in this volume are from the New Revised Standard Version of the Bible, copyright 1989, Division of Christian Education of the National Council of the Churches of Christ in the United States of America. Used by permission. All rights reserved.

Images on pages 108, 110, 124–125, 132–135 courtesy of Anna Marie Texter, Perkasie, PA.

Library of Congress Cataloging-in-Publication Data

Crisci, Elizabeth W.
  Celebrate good times! : 26 complete parties / Elizabeth Whitney Crisci.
    p. cm.
  ISBN 0-8170-1486-1 (alk. paper)
  1. Parties—Religious aspects—Christianity. I. Title.
  BV4517.5.C75 2005
  793.2—dc22   2005019378
Printed in the U.S.A.

13 12 11 10 09 08 07 06 05
10 9 8 7 6 5 4 3 2 1

Dedication

This book is dedicated to all fun-loving Christians and to my devoted pastor-husband, who has enabled me to plan and execute many parties all our married life. O, that all churches would take time for relaxation and fun during their calendar year—for the purpose of good Christian fellowship as well as for drawing in new people. God bless all joy-filled Christians!

Contents

Introduction

Section One: Seasonal Parties

Section Two: Small Group Parties

Section Three: Large Group Parties

Section Four: Outreach Parties

Introduction

Parties are fun, and they offer a sense of community and joy to all who gather, whether the event is inspired by a holiday or just a desire to infuse some excitement into a "same old" month. There are many worldly occasions that leave God out of our lives and celebrations. Therefore, it is wise and necessary to have parties that nurture our faith as well as our need for fun. There will be lots of fun awaiting those who participate in parties, and others will see how much fun God's people can have.

How often should you host a party? There's no reason for church groups to have "fun" only once a year. Set a goal to make get-togethers frequent and memorable. If parties are enjoyable, with plenty of opportunity for people to get to know each other better, guests will make future parties a priority, and they will be willing to help plan and create the fun. In the process, God's people will bond together in friendships and joy.

Let each of these parties serve that purpose and pray that God will direct your plans, and that the experience will motivate people to join in planning and hosting fellowship events.

What Makes a Great Party?

Film director Peter Bogdanovich says a great movie is one with one or two great scenes and no bad scenes. A great party is the same way. To use this book . . .

1. Look through the party activities, envisioning how *your* group would respond to each one. Make sure that each activity is fast-paced, and plan to change games before people become bored.

2. Choose activities that your group would truly enjoy and plan a mix of lighthearted and meaningful activities. Substitute activities that don't work for your group with your own or leave more time for conversation. (That's the part of most gatherings you like best anyway, right?)

3. Try to determine which one or two aspects in the party plans you think will be the most memorable for your group—the part of the evening they'll think of fondly in the days after the event is over. Give those features of the party the most time.

And consider . . .

■ *Pre-planning:* One person alone might be very capable of (and even prefer) producing the entire party, but working with a team has its advantages. With the goal of each member of the planning team approaching this as a ministry worthy of time, energy, and prayer in mind, you can divide event responsibilities among persons or even among committees. Select a party chair who, in turn, can set up party committees: publicity, refreshments, game leaders, greeters, devotional leader, decorators, set up, and clean up. List everything that must be done in advance; publicity, for example, needs advance preparation. Select a game leader who will be excited, which, in turn, will enthuse everyone else. Game leaders need to make or find all the props in advance.

■ *Publicity:* Send post cards for each occasion at least two weeks in advance. Include date, time, place, and the title of the event. Include an eye-catching design. Place several posters around the church with similar information. Have parties listed in church bulletins and newsletters.

■ *Refreshments:* Refreshment choices will depend on how the event is funded. If an entry fee will be charged, food can be purchased in bulk at a discount store. If each party will be funded through the church budget, you might ask guests to bring a dessert to share, giving them suggestions that go along with the theme. There are many ways to determine who brings what. You can post a sign-up sheet and have families bring what they want or even assign last name initials to bring beverages, etc. To ensure variety from party to party, you can assign a theme for the desserts or specific types of beverages. Some planners even distribute self-explanatory dessert recipes to selected guests.

■ *Fellowship: Celebrate Good Times!* was planned to make party preparation and giving easy and meaningful. The suggested programs are designed to nurture Christian fellowship and to help church members reach out to those who might not come to a church service but would be comfortable attending a party. After a happy experience at a party, some non-church-attendees might feel comfortable visiting a worship service. Be sure to back up each event with prayer that all who attend might be strengthened in faith and bonded in fellowship. May you be blessed as you plan gatherings that strengthen your church, enhance fellowship, and bring honor to God.

SECTION ONE

Seasonal Parties

The word *holidays* reminds us that holidays once were *holy* days, set aside to honor God, recall the historical events that formed us, celebrate creation, and renew people. The purpose of these seasonal parties is to celebrate occasions in a Christian atmosphere and to have pleasurable gatherings marked by fun, relaxation, and strengthening of relationships.

PARTY 1
New Year's Happenings

GEARED FOR:
ADULTS IN SMALL GROUPS OR LARGE GROUPS

Prizes (pick one or two kinds, or have a variety set out for winners to choose from): candy, small calendars, calendar stickers, Happy New Year hats or noisemakers, etc.

Do ahead:
- Read "What Makes a Great Party?" on pages ix–xi.
- Select activities, prepare materials, and plan the refreshments.
- Print out "Three Minute Interview" questions from page 3 on newsprint

Welcome Table and Opening Activity
Supplies needed:
- nametags
- markers
- "The Three-Minute Interview" questions

As the people arrive, it is wise to have an activity to keep them busy, yet free to talk to others. Have people walk around the room saying their birth month over and over. When a guest finds someone else also saying that same month, they become a team. If a guest cannot find a partner in this way, the guest can join an

▼ ▼ ▼ ▼ ▼ ▼ ▼ ▼ ▼ ▼ ▼ ▼ ▼ ▼ ▼ ▼ ▼ ▼

established couple to become a trio or team up with a person born the month before or after.

Introduce the "Three-Minute Interview" activity. Have pairs share for six to ten minutes. Flick the lights on and off half-way through to signal interviewer/interviewee switch. If time permits, have a few people share something they found out during the Three-Minute Interview. You may choose to prolong this activity by having guests form new groups if many guests are still arriving. *Suggested "Three-Minute Interview" questions:*

- Where were you born?
- What is your favorite snack food?
- Who is your greatest hero/heroine?
- What three words describe you?
- What was the last good book you read or movie you saw?
- Which Bible character are you most like?
- What is your favorite hobby?
- If you had a day to do anything you wanted, what would it be?

Activity: What a Year!
Supplies needed:
- copies of "What a Year" (1 copy per 20 or so guests)

Gather the people in circles of up to 20 chairs. Then explain the game. A person designated as "It" stands in the center with the bag. "It" points to someone seated in the circle and then reads a date from "What a Year," *Celebrate Good Times* page 4. If a category, such as "sports" or "invention" is given, "It" identifies that as he or she reads the date. The chosen person correctly names the event connected with the date or becomes "It."

▼ ▼ ▼ ▼ ▼ ▼ ▼ ▼ ▼ ▼ ▼ ▼ ▼ ▼ ▼ ▼ ▼ ▼

"WHAT A YEAR!"

1492: Christopher Columbus arrived in the Caribbean.

1620: Pilgrims landed in what would become Plymouth, Massachusetts.

1776: The Continental Congress signed The Declaration of Independence.

1779: George Washington became the first president of the United States.

1788: The Constitution of the United States was ratified.

1800 invention: Volta—the electric battery

1804: The Lewis and Clark Expedition began.

1808: Congress prohibited the importing of enslaved Africans.

1861: The Civil War began.

1863: Emancipation Proclamation was issued.

1865: The Thirteenth Amendment, abolishing slavery, was ratified.

1876 sports: the American League of baseball was founded.

1879 invention: Alexander Graham Bell—the telephone.

1879 invention: Thomas Edison—the incandescent bulb.

1917: The United States entered World War I.

1927: Charles Lindberg flew across the Atlantic.

1929: The U.S. Stock Market crashed.

1933: President Franklin Delano Roosevelt introduced The New Deal.

1941: The United States entered World War II.

1947 sports: Jackie Robinson joined the Brooklyn Dodgers.

1948 invention: Bell Labs—the transistor

1950: The United States entered the Korean War.

1954: The Supreme Court ruled that segregated schools are unconstitutional.

1955: Rosa Parks refused to give up her seat on a bus in Montgomery, Alabama.

1963: President John F. Kennedy was assassinated.

1964: The U.S. entered the Vietnam War/Congress passed a Civil Rights Act.

1968: Dr. Martin Luther King Jr. was assassinated.

1969: U.S. astronauts landed on the Moon.

1979 sports: Pirates won the World Series/Steelers won the Super Bowl.

1981: Sandra Day O'Connor became the first female Supreme Court Justice.

2001: The United States suffered the 9/11 terrorist attacks.

Activity: My Resolutions

Supplies needed:

■ sample "My Resolutions" acrostics on poster
board or overhead

■ paper and pencils for each guest

Do ahead:

■ Print out the sample "My Resolutions" acrostics on poster
board or overhead slides.

■ As an alternative, you may want to type "New Year" down the
left-hand side of page two times and print or photocopy sheets for
your guests to use.

Give each guest paper and pencil and show the sample acrostics.
Say: *"You have a chance to make two sets of resolutions. One can
be serious. The other can be a list you might resolve if you were
taking cues from classic TV shows, such as The Waltons, I Love
Lucy, The Cosby Show, Mister Rogers, Green Acres, Little House
on the Prairie, Happy Days, and Perry Mason. Think up one resolution to correspond to each letter."* Give the guests time to create their own original resolutions then allow time for sharing.

"My Resolutions" acrostic 1:

N - No gossip   Y - Yearn to introduce others to Jesus
E - Entertain neighbor   E - Expect answers to prayer
W- Work harder   A - Apply the Bible more
                             R - Remember Birthdays

"My Resolutions" acrostic 2:

N - Never overlook foul play ("Murder, She Wrote")

E - Explore new worlds ("Star Trek")

W - Wear pearls during housework ("Father Knows Best")

Y - Yell at your hubby ("Home Improvement")

E - Eat more "Flek" ("Mork & Mindy")

A - Always wish your family goodnight ("The Waltons")

R - Run, Forrest, run! (*Forrest Gump*)

Activity: I Resolve

Everyone sits in a circle. One person says, *"This New Year, I resolve to _____,"* making a short resolution (such as "sing a solo," "walk to church," "take the stairs," etc.). The next person repeats the previous resolution and adds a new one. The next person in the circle must repeat the first two and add a new one, and so it goes until the list gets impossible to remember. If someone can't repeat the previous resolutions, that person is out.

Activity: Months and Days

A person designated as "It" stands in the center of the circle, points to someone, says the name of a month, and counts to five. Before "It" gets to five, the person pointed at has to say the number of days in that month. If February is called, use the number of days in the coming year or accept either 28 or 29. If the person doesn't respond correctly before the count of five, that person becomes "It." This is more difficult than it would seem, because it must be done so quickly. Keep the game going fast. Months with 30 days: April, June, September, and November. Months with 31 days: January, March, May, July, August, October, and December.

Activity: New Year's Achievement Awards

Supplies needed:

■ gold award seals (gold foil seals are found at office supply stores); four per person

■ 1/2-inch wide strips of red paper or wide ribbon (for wrapping packages) cut in four-inch lengths, with one end of each cut with v-shaped notch; four per person

■ paper and pencil, one per person (included in handout packet)

■ black fine-point permanent marker, one per group

■ plastic sandwich bags to gather craft supplies, one per person

Ask guests to gather in groups of approximately four or as families. Explain: *"You will be making your own awards to celebrate a personal achievement. "Personal" means important to you! Perhaps it's making it to the sports club twenty days in a row; teaching a child to read; giving up biting your nails; being cancer-free for a year; tutoring someone in English as a second language; or keeping a journal for more than a month. The only criterion is that it is important to you! Jot down at least four achievements on your blank paper. Then choose four to make into awards. To do this, take four gold seals and four ribbon pieces. Peel one of the gold seals off the backing, stick two red ribbons onto the sticker so that two ends make a 30-degree angle, and stick another seal on the back side of them. (The sticky sides of the two gold seals will stick together.) You're making a two-sided award. Write one achievement on one side, either on the gold seal or on the ribbon, and another on the other side. Then make another set and write your other two achievements on them. Place them in your desk or bureau. When you come across them, they'll encourage you throughout the coming year."*

Bible Emphasis

Sing a couple of songs such as "O God Our Help in Ages Past" and/or Bill Gaither's "The Longer I Serve Him." Have the leader prepare a brief talk on Psalm 100.

Ask the guests to offer words of praise to God for the past year. Read Psalm 100. Then reread: "Worship the LORD with gladness." Continue by saying: "*Verse 2a is a good resolution for the new year. How do we worship God? Rick Warren puts it simply: 'Anything you do that brings pleasure to God is an act of worship'* (The Purpose Driven Life, 64). Invite sharing about ways we bring pleasure to God. Conclude with a chorus of Bill Gaither's "I Will Serve Thee, Because I Love Thee" or the well-known "Make Me a Blessing."

Refreshments

Serve several decorated cakes (perhaps a chocolate, a lemon, and a spice cake) with "Happy New Year" printed on them. Serve ice cream and fruit punch.

OR

Serve classic treats with a sign noting the year they came on the market. Church members can sign up for foods such as Twinkies (1933); PopTarts (1964); Krispy Kreme Donuts (1937); Diet Coke (1982); Classic Coke (1986); Betty Crocker Cake Mix (1937); Jelly Bellies (1978); Jell-O Jigglers (1990); etc. Decorate the table with cutouts from the boxes or with nostalgic ads found in old magazines or on the Internet. To find the inaugural years for other foods you wish to serve, consult the Internet.

▼ ▼ ▼ ▼ ▼ ▼ ▼ ▼ ▼ ▼ ▼ ▼ ▼ ▼ ▼ ▼ ▼

PARTY 2
Celebrating Martin Luther King Jr. Day

Appropriate for February, Black History Month

GEARED FOR: ADULTS IN SMALL GROUPS OR LARGE GROUPS

Prizes (pick one or two kinds, or have a variety set out for winners to choose from): candy, birthday party goody-bag trinkets

Do ahead:
■ Read "What Makes a Great Party?" on pages ix–xi.
■ Select activities, prepare materials, and plan the refreshments.
■ Think about diversity when inviting guests.

Welcome Table and Opening Activity
Supplies needed:
■ nametags
■ markers and pens
■ copy of "People and Dates" for each guest

As people arrive, hand out "People and Dates" and encourage working in groups. When everyone is done, review the answers. Answers to matching are: 1e; 2h; 3g; 4b; 5d; 6a; 7c; 8f. Answers to date identification are: 1. 1963; 2. 1773; 3. 1992; 4. 1772; 5. 1949.

▼ ▼ ▼ ▼ ▼ ▼ ▼ ▼ ▼ ▼ ▼ ▼ ▼ ▼ ▼ ▼ ▼ ▼

PEOPLE AND DATES

Draw lines from the person to his or her accomplishment:

1. Mae Jemison   a. first woman millionaire through her
                                      own business

2. Benjamin Oliver Davis   b. first bishop in the African Methodist
                                      Episcopal Church

3. Crispus Attucks   c. first African American to win Masters golf
                                      tournament

4. Richard Allen   d. first African American to win the Academy
                                      Award for Best Actress

5. Halle Berry   e. first African American astronaut

6. Madame C. J. Walker   f. first black senator

7. Tiger Woods   g. first casualty for American Independence

8. Hiram R. Revels   h. first black general in the U. S. Army

Circle the correct date answer:

1. Martin Luther King Jr. gave his "I Have a Dream" speech in
      1949   1960   1963

2. Phillis Wheatley became the first notable black woman poet in English in
      1773   1873   1972

3. Arizona approved Martin Luther King Jr. Day as a legal holiday in
      1956   1988   1992

4. Jean-Baptiste-Point Du Sable became the first settler in Chicago in
      1654   1772   1875

5. Gwendolyn Brooks, the first African American to win the Pulitzer Prize in
Poetry, was awarded the prize in
      1943   1949   1975

Activity: Remembrances of the Past

Read the following story about The Reverend Dr. Martin Luther King Jr. Lead a discussion about race relations when party guests were children, young people, in the workplace, at college, etc. Ask one or two guests to be prepared to start the discussion.

A Baptist pastor, Martin Luther King Jr. (1929–1968), is best known for his leadership in the civil rights movement and, particularly, for his commitment to a nonviolent approach to securing equal rights for all.

King graduated from high school at the age of 15 and earned a B.A. degree from Morehouse College (Atlanta) in 1948. He studied theology at Crozer Theological Seminary in Chester, Pennsyl-vania, where he was elected president of his senior class. King went on to study at Boston University, receiving a doctorate in 1955.

In December of 1955, he accepted the leadership of the Montgomery, Alabama, bus boycott, a nonviolent demonstration that lasted 382 days and ended in December of 1956 when the Supreme Court declared unconstitutional laws requiring segregation on busses.

In 1957, King was elected president of the Southern Christian Leadership conference, a major arm of the civil rights movement. In his leadership position, he combined Christian ideals with nonviolent techniques practiced by Gandhi. Between 1957 and 1968, he traveled more than six million miles and spoke more than 2,500 times protesting injustice. He was arrested more than twenty times and assaulted on at least four occasions.

At the age of 35, King became the youngest person to receive the Nobel Peace Prize. He turned the prize money over to causes supporting the civil rights movement. King died in Memphis, Tennessee on April 4, 1968 as a result of an assassin's bullet. He'd traveled to Memphis to lead a protest march for striking garbage workers.

Bible Emphasis: True Unity

Sing several songs about love and unity, such as "They Will Know We are Christians by Our Love" or "Blest Be the Tie." Read John 17:22-23. Encourage sharing about the way race relations have improved and things for which participants are thankful. Also encourage sharing about ways each one of us contributes to disharmony. Remind everyone that the vision of unity found in John 17:22-23 won't happen by magic; it will happen when everyone takes responsibility. Invite a time of private prayer for forgiveness for the ways we divide ourselves and offer a closing prayer, thanking God for the work of Dr. King and others and asking for courage to seek justice and unity.

Refreshments

Set the table to look like a birthday party. Serve a variety of sandwich halves and a large sheet cake with candles that spell out "M.L.K." or "We Shall Overcome." Serve coffee, tea, and punch.

▼ ▼ ▼ ▼ ▼ ▼ ▼ ▼ ▼ ▼ ▼ ▼ ▼ ▼ ▼ ▼ ▼ ▼ ▼

PARTY 3
Celebration of Valentines

GEARED FOR: ADULTS IN
SMALL GROUPS OR LARGE GROUPS

Prizes (pick one or two kinds, or have a variety set out for winners to choose from): small candy hearts of various sizes, heart-shaped votive candles, etc.

Do ahead:
- Read "What Makes a Great Party?" on pages ix–xi.
- Select activities, prepare materials, and plan the refreshments.
- Write or find a story for "Heart Tale."

Welcome Table and Opening Activity
Supplies needed:
- nametags
- markers
- copies of "Valentine Tracker," one per person
- pencils, one per person

As people arrive, have them complete the Valentine Tracker and invite them to get signatures of people who fit each statement. After everyone has arrived, have everyone sit down and share discoveries. Give a prize to the person with the most points.

VALENTINE TRACKER

I sent a valentine overseas by e-mail or letter.   (3 points)

I gave a handmade valentine to someone.   (3 points)

I received a heart-shaped box of chocolates.   (5 points)

I went out to dinner for St. Valentine's Day.   (1 point)

I bought a valentine for a family member.   (4 points)

I wore red to celebrate St. Valentine's Day.   (1 point)

I still have a valentine that was given to me
over ten years ago.   (5 points)

10 POINTS EXTRA CREDIT:
I possess a valentine card that is older than anyone in the room.

▼ ▼ ▼ ▼ ▼ ▼ ▼ ▼ ▼ ▼ ▼ ▼ ▼ ▼ ▼ ▼ ▼ ▼

Activity: Broken Hearts

Supplies needed:

■ red poster board
■ several styles of romantic wrapping paper
■ glue

Cut heart (one per each five guests) from red poster board. Cover the white side of the heart with romantic wrapping paper, using a different style for each heart, then cut into 10–15 pieces to make a puzzle. As guests arrive, give one or more pieces from the same heart to each guest. At a signal, they must find their team members and put the puzzle together to make a heart. If you wish, have each team choose a love song to perform for the group. Give each team member who completed the puzzle a prize.

Activity: Heart Tale

Supplies needed:

■ a story that frequently uses "love" and "valentine"

Divide group into two teams: men and women. Have each group decide on a love song they will sing. Every time the storyteller uses the word *love*, all the women will break out into a phrase or two of the love song. Every time the storyteller uses the word *valentine*, the men sing part of the song of their choice. Sometimes the teller can substitute a different word for *love* to trick the singers. It might be something like this: "A long time ago, Joe fell in love with a girl named Anne in his algebra class. He was really in love. Everywhere he looked he saw valentines. He decided to make her a valentine that was one big valentine and many little valentines. In the center he wrote . . . *Anne.* He couldn't wait to give her the card to express his . . . regard. He couldn't keep his mind on the teacher's comments."

Activity: Heart Throbs

Supplies needed:

■ large cardboard heart

■ love songs, played on a CD player, tape recorder, or piano (optional)

Have a large cardboard heart, heart candy box, or a red heart-shaped pillow. The guests sit in a circle and pass the heart around the circle. Play some love songs and stop the music unexpectedly. If you don't have music, you can have the group spell out *valentine* as the heart goes around. (Each pass of the heart becomes another letter.) When the music stops or the word ends, the person holding the heart must sing part of a love song.

Activity: Valentine I.Q.

Supplies needed:

■ sheets of paper with the numbers 1–10 listed vertically and the word *VALENTINE* across the top, one per person

■ pencils, one for each person

Pass out papers and pencils. Explain that *E* and *N* may be used twice in a word (for example, eve or nine) because they appear twice in the word *Valentine.* At a signal, have guests try to create as many words of three letters or more as they can, using the letters in *Valentine.* Whichever person finds 10 words first calls out "Valentine!" and reads off his or her list. If the words are acceptable, that guest is declared the winner and receives a prize. Then you might continue for the second and third prizes.

▼ ▼ ▼ ▼ ▼ ▼ ▼ ▼ ▼ ▼ ▼ ▼ ▼ ▼ ▼ ▼ ▼

Craft: Comic Valentines

Do Ahead:

■ Make a sample "Comic Valentine" and create forms to trace for the envelopes

■ Type up and copy one set of "Comic Valentines" instructions per table or print instructions out on newsprint

Supplies needed:

■ past issues of the Sunday comics

■ construction paper or card stock in primary colors

■ glue sticks or rubber cement (not bottled glue)

■ scissors

■ blank white paper

■ envelopes to open up and trace

■ felt-tip pens

■ pens, for signing cards

■ instructions for "Comic Valentines"

■ sample "Comic Valentine"

■ cardboard patterns traced from your sample envelope larger envelopes addressed to homebound people, hospital patients, and friends who are isolated caring for ill or aging relatives

Instructions for "Comic Valentines":

1. Select a panel from Sunday comics.

2. Cut the panel out and paste it onto construction paper or card-stock.

3. Draw a comic strip balloon and write in a new caption.

4. Sign the card on the back.

5. Trace an envelope onto an interesting part of the comics and cut out. (The formula for the envelope is: length-2½ times the width of the card; width-length of card plus 1 inch.)

6. Trim top of envelope into shape of a flap (see photo on page 18).

7. Fold into envelope and paste (see photo below).

8. Cut a "balloon" out of white paper and paste it onto the front of the envelope for the recipient's name.

9. Place Valentine card inside and lightly paste flaps.

Explain to the party guests: *"The original St. Valentine was a Christian martyr who wrote letters to his jailer's child. He signed the letters 'Your Valentine.' Today we're going to make 'Comic Valentines.' Make as many as you wish plus one to be sent out. Volunteers are also needed to address large envelopes for mailing the extra valentines to church friends who are homebound, ill, or in nursing homes."* Review instructions and direct guests to tables supplied with valentines materials. Arrange for volunteers to mail out the larger envelopes. Everyone who helps gets a prize.

▼ ▼ ▼ ▼ ▼ ▼ ▼ ▼ ▼ ▼ ▼ ▼ ▼ ▼ ▼ ▼ ▼ ▼

Bible Emphasis

Say to the guests: *"Author Gary Chapman has pinpointed five different ways we show and receive love: acts of service, physical touch, words of affirmation, quality time, and giving gifts. Each of us has one primary love language—possibly two. Our primary love language is the language we're most likely to use to show our love. It is easy to see these five love languages in Jesus' own life. And Jesus calls us to show love, as it says in 1 John 4: 'Dear friends, let us love one another, for love comes from God. Everyone who loves has been born of God and knows God.' (NIV) Knowing your love language may explain a lot about you. What is your favorite language to express love? To receive love?*

 Allow people time to share. Close with a hymn as your prayer. Good possibilities include: "My Jesus, I Love Thee," "Love Lifted Me," More Love to Thee," and "They Will Know We Are Christians by Our Love."

Refreshments

Serve heart-shaped sandwiches, a relish tray, chips with a dip in a heart-shaped bowl, heart-shaped cakes, coffee, tea, and punch.

PARTY 4
Easter Party

GEARED FOR:
ADULTS IN SMALL GROUPS OR LARGE GROUPS

Prizes (pick one or two kinds, or have a variety set out for winners to choose from): filled Easter eggs, miniature baskets, Easter candy, etc.

Do ahead:
- Read "What Makes a Great Party?" on pages ix–xi.
- Select activities, prepare materials, and plan the refreshments.

Welcome Table and Opening Activity:
Supplies needed:
- nametags
- markers
- nice stationery, one piece per guest
- pens, one for each guest

As the people arrive, it is wise to have an activity to keep them busy, yet free to talk to others. As they enter, give each person a sheet of attractive paper and a pen. Ask them to get as many autographs as possible. The purpose is two-fold: to get people talking, and to get to know different guests. The one with the most autographs gets a prize.

Activity: Easter Greetings

Supplies needed:

■ Easter cards with Christian messages, as many as you wish to send

■ pens, one per person

■ stamps

■ addresses of homebound persons, nursing home residents, or recent visitors

Pass out pens to those who need them. Pass around the Easter cards, and ask everyone to sign them and add a brief word of encouragement, if they desire. Ask for volunteers to help address envelopes and prepare them to send to homebound persons, nursing home residents, or recent visitors.

Activity: Now You See Them . . .

Supplies needed:

■ tray with ten items to symbolize the resurrection, such as a cross, a gospel tract, thirty dimes, a silk lily, a picture of an empty tomb, a crown of thorns, a stone, a palm branch, a nail, a sunrise picture (or anything else that applies)

■ paper, one piece per guest

■ pencils or pens, one per guest

Arrange the ten items on a tray, but keep the tray hidden. Hand out pencils and paper. Display the tray to the group for a minute and then remove the tray again. Ask guests to write down the ten items. Those who remember all ten get a prize.

Activity: Hot Eggs
Supplies needed:
■ three plastic eggs for every thirty people (glue the eggs shut)
■ taped music and player

Ask everyone to sit in circles of no more than thirty people. Have three plastic eggs and give them to different people in a circle. At the sound of music, the egg holders pass the eggs to the right with their feet. When the music stops, those with the eggs must stand, do a "silly deed," and sit down, ready to pass the eggs again when the music starts. Have other circles of guests do the game at the same time.
Suggested "silly deeds":
1. Sing "Mary Had a Little Lamb."
2. Hop on right foot for ten seconds.
3. Turn around twice.
4. Pat your head and rub your stomach.
5. Run or walk around the outside of the circle three times.
6. Recite something you memorized in school.
7. Say something in a foreign language.
8. Share a high school experience.

Game: Easter Egg Hunt
Supplies needed:
■ dozens of small plastic Easter eggs, only five of which have Scripture references written on the outside and contain the verse

written out on a piece of paper. The verses are: John 11:25, Mark 16:6, Luke 24:5-7, Matthew 28:5-6, and Acts 17:18.

■ Easter basket tied with pink bow
■ Easter basket tied with blue bow

Before the party, place the appropriate Scripture verse inside the egg that has its reference on the outside. Then hide all the Easter eggs.

At the party say, *"It's sometimes said that mothers are best at finding things. Let's find out. We're going to have an Easter egg hunt. All the eggs found by the women go in the pink basket. All the eggs found by the men go in the blue."* Allow people to start looking. After five minutes, call everyone back to the circle to deposit their eggs in the appropriate baskets. Congratulate the winning side and distribute prizes to the winners. Remove the five Scripture eggs for use in the devotional.

Bible Emphasis

Supplies needed:

■ five plastic Easter eggs with Scripture verses related to the resurrection

Sing three Easter songs, such as "Because He Lives," "Christ the Lord Is Risen Today," and "He Arose." Toss the five Easter eggs with Scripture verses to five guests and ask them to read the verses aloud. A speaker could speak on the centrality of Christ's resurrection to the

Christian faith. This is an excellent opportunity to make a clear presentation of the gospel or to share peronal faith journeys with one another.

Refreshments

Serve fancy sandwiches and a fruit tray. Have egg-shaped sugar cookies with pastel icings and an Easter cake decorated with the phrase, "He Is Risen." Serve coffee, tea, and punch.

PARTY 5
Cinco de Mayo

GEARED FOR:
ADULTS COUPLES, ADULT SINGLES,
OR A COLLEGE GROUP

Cinco de Mayo is the anniversary of the Battle of Pueblo, where Mexico defeated Maximillian's French forces in 1862. Celebrated more widely in the United States than in Mexico because the commander of the Mexican forces, Gen. Ignacios Zaragoza, was born in Godiad, Texas, the holiday has made its way to the White House Rose Garden.

Do Ahead:
■ Read "What Makes a Great Party?" on pages ix–xi.
■ If before Easter you know that you are going to do this party, look for and purchase wax *cascarones*, eggs filled with confetti which are now sold in many chain grocery and party stores. If you miss the Easter season, look for them on the Internet.
■ Find church members who will cook Mexican dishes. It would add a lot to the event if two or three people practice making fresh tortillas with you so that guests can make their own at the party.
■ Start looking for portable single electric burners to borrow. It may help to put a notice in the church bulletin.
■ Begin to look early for a speaker for this event. See "Bible Emphasis" for suggestions.

■ Be sure to note on the invitation and the publicity materials that families and individuals must RSVP for the party. You'll need to know what items guests can donate to the party and how many supplies to have prepared ahead of time.

■ Provide a list of taco or tortilla fixings and have a sign-up sheet so that you are sure to get a variety and know ahead of time which items you'll need to purchase.

¡Hola! (Hello) Welcome Table and Opening Activity

Supplies needed:

■ nametags with *¡Hola!* written on them

■ markers

■ Mexican-style music and decorations (Spanish-language newspapers are inexpensive decorations and can be used as wrapping paper or placemats).

■ music player

■ *cascaron* eggs, one for every two people

This is a good outdoor game. Have guests form pairs. Line up pairs across from each other. Give one person in each pair a *cascaron*. Guests stand toe to toe and toss the egg to each other. After both people have had a turn tossing and catching the egg, they each take one step farther apart. Then they each toss and catch the egg again. Partners keep moving apart one step after each successful round. When the eggs are dropped or caught too roughly (especially during a long toss), they will break open. When a pair's egg cracks, that pair is out of the game. The pair that moves farthest apart without their egg cracking is the winner.

▼ ▼ ▼ ▼ ▼ ▼ ▼ ▼ ▼ ▼ ▼ ▼ ▼ ▼ ▼ ▼ ▼ ▼

Program: Ultimate Tacos Fiesta

Create a taco buffet. An excellent resource is *The Well-Filled Tortilla*, by Victoria Wise and Susanna Hoffman. Have different guests bring fixings, including: seasoned ground beef, shredded beef, shredded chicken, black beans, refried beans, different kinds of shredded cheese, chopped tomatoes, diced sun-dried tomatoes, sour cream, diced red and green peppers, diced Spanish onion, diced black olives, minced jalapeno peppers (display with a warning sign), chopped peanuts, guacamole, various styles of tortilla shells, taco sauces and fresh salsa.

Consider having guests make their own tortillas (instructions below) and consider flan, which many grocery stores sell frozen or as a mix, for desert. Simple recipes for flan are also available in Mexican cookbooks and on the Internet.

Activity: Make-Your-Own Tortillas

Supplies needed:

- portable single electric burners, two or three
- extension cords (make sure the burners won't blow a fuse if all are on the same circuit)
- skillets, one per burner
- spatula for removing tortilla
- wooden cutting boards, one per burner
- hand wipes for wiping hands after guests make tortillas
- bowls, one per helper making dough
- cotton dish towels to cover dough
- 5 pound bag of flour
- bottle of vegetable oil
- water
- salt

■ extra, store-bought tortillas so that guests can have more than one and for those who prefer not to make their own

A few hours before the party, have some helpers make tortilla dough. For 12 tortillas: Mix three cups of flour with 1/3 cup of vegetable oil with a fork or your fingers until the dough is crumbly. Spoon 1 teaspoon of salt into a cup of warm water and stir it until the salt dissolves. Pour the salt water over the flour mixture. Knead the dough until it seems elastic (3–5 minutes). Place the dough in the bowl, cover it with a cloth and let rest for at least an hour.

Right before the party, make a long rope with each dough ball. Cut each rope into 12 equal pieces, and cover the pieces with damp cloths.

When it's time for the party, set up the portable burners on one side of a long table. Place a cutting board in front of each burner. Set the burners on medium high and cover each with a flat, ungreased skillet. Have each helper posted at a burner and invite guests to make their own tortillas as follows:

■ Working on the cutting board surface, form a dough piece into a ball and then pat it into a thin tortilla about 8 inches across.

■ Place the tortilla onto the pan and warm each side for at least thirty seconds.

■ Carefully remove the tortilla with a spatula.

■ Fill at the taco bar.

Bible Emphasis

Here are a few options for this event's devotional:

1. Invite a friend of Mexican heritage (perhaps a person who was born in Mexico) to present a folktale or personal account from childhood.

▼ ▼ ▼ ▼ ▼ ▼ ▼ ▼ ▼ ▼ ▼ ▼ ▼ ▼ ▼ ▼ ▼

2. Invite someone who has traveled to Mexico to talk and show pictures, slides, or video from the trip.

3. Invite a former missionary or one on home assignment from Mexico to share his or her experiences.

4. Invite an ESL (English as a Second Language) teacher from a public school to field questions about what he or she likes best about the job and what it's like for immigrant children in the community. Ask the ESL teacher to bring names of any support programs that welcome volunteers. If your church is part of an ESL program for adults, some representatives could come to share. Ask him or her to teach the group John 3:16 in Spanish.

End the evening with prayer for our neighboring country Mexico and for those of Mexican heritage in your own community.

▼ ▼ ▼ ▼ ▼ ▼ ▼ ▼ ▼ ▼ ▼ ▼ ▼ ▼ ▼ ▼ ▼ ▼

PARTY 6
Fourth of July Picnic

GEARED FOR:
FAMILIES, SMALL GROUPS OR LARGE GROUPS

Prizes (pick one or two kinds, or have a variety set out for winners to choose from): candy, extra bubble wrap (see "Virtual Firecrackers" activity), or miniature flags. Good prizes for the dessert contest are 3D fireworks glasses. These are disposable eyeglasses for fireworks viewing that are available in some party stores or through the Internet.

Do ahead:
■ Read "What Makes a Great Party?" on pages ix–xi.
■ Plan and promote the parent/child dessert making contest, announcing the prize categories: Best Use of Fruit, Chocolatiest, Best No-bake Dessert, Best Decorated, and Most Creative. (optional, see Barbecue and Dessert Contest)

Welcome Table and Opening Activity:
Supplies needed:
■ nametags
■ black markers

■ red, blue, green, orange markers or dot labels. As guests arrive, draw or stick a red, blue, green, or orange mark or dot on their nametags. Make sure young children get the same color dot as a parent.

■ adaptations for a large group: portable microphone or megaphone and a whistle

■ grocery bags, one per teams of two or three

■ "Scavenger Hunt" list that you compose, one per team

As everyone arrives, hand each one a bag with a list of things to find. Send people forth in twos or threes to find the items. Don't let any new people go by themselves but team them up with people who could become new friends. After fifteen minutes call everyone together. Give a prize to the person (or persons) with the most items.

The following are some possible scavenger hunt items: pine needles, a live bug, a round stone, a rusty nail, a candy wrapper, a broken pencil, a sock, five smooth stones, a paper clip, a penny, a plastic cup, and a partly burned piece of charcoal. You will need to adapt your particular list to the items you could find relatively easily in your locale.

Simultaneous Outdoor Games

Supplies needed (depending on game selection):

■ Scrabble set and picnic table
■ Pictionary and picnic table
■ croquet set
■ volleyball and net
■ softball equipment and bases
■ jigsaw puzzle (if available, outdoor scene from your own locale)
■ horseshoes or bocci ball set (lawn bowling)

- basketball (if a hoop is available)
- large round foam ball (for modified dodge ball)
- whistle or bull horn

Depending on the size of your group, select five activities that can be played for a while before moving to another. If children are included, plan games they can enjoy with adults. Guests should have a red, blue, green, or orange dot or mark on their nametags. Young children should have the same color dot as a parent. Have red people become one team and blue people another, etc. There will be games in which players from two teams will be on the same side.

Have one leader at each sports game to get things started and to referee. When play begins, guests can join any game they choose, but after about 20 minutes the leader should blow a whistle and have everyone with reds and blues switch games. After another 20 minutes, oranges and greens find new games. After about an hour and a half, stop the games. If you want to find an overall winner, instruct people to tell the coordinator which color teams win which games. Give prizes to the winners and move on to Relay Races and Firecracker Hunt.

Scrabble, Pictionary, and the puzzle can be set up on picnic tables. Croquet needs a leader who can explain the rules because many people have not played this fun game. Scaled-down games of volleyball and softball can be played with an improvised net and bases. Plan to play basketball if there is a hoop nearby. Horseshoes or bocci ball (lawn bowling) won't need an ongoing leader as long as the remaining players explain the rules to new players. For a simple, non-threatening version of dodge ball, use a large foam ball. Make a circle and have three people in the middle. The people on the outside throw the ball, trying to hit someone in the center, avoiding the face. If a player hits someone, he or she gets into the center, and the person hit joins the circle.

Relay Races
Supplies needed:
■ 2-liter bottle filled with flour (optional)
■ small candy prizes

Before the picnic, locate an open space for running. Just before the games, squirt flour from the bottle to mark the start and finish lines. Guests should have a red, blue, green, or orange dot on their nametags. Young children should have the same color dot as a parent. Using the colors on the nametags, divide into two teams (two colors on each side). Run races with running, walking, hopping, skipping, crawling on all fours, or walking backwards. Award prizes to race winners.

"Firecracker" Hunt
Supplies needed:
■ toilet paper tube
■ construction paper
■ string for "firecracker" (directions below)

Make a fake firecracker from an old toilet paper tube covered in red construction paper. Trail a piece of string out of one end like a fuse. Hide it in an inconspicuous place adjacent to the picnic area. Send everyone off to find it but not to touch it. Players should observe the spot and silently hurry back to the picnic area, trying not to give away the location to other players. When most of the people have found it, have the first person who found it retrieve the firecracker, revealing its hiding place. Give prizes to the first three finders.

Virtual Firecrackers

Supplies needed:

■ "foot-sized" squares of large bubble wrap, several for each child
■ recycling bin

It's easy to get all the bang of firecrackers without the mess or danger. This activity is a good way to get a second use out of bubble wrap before recycling it. Take the children to a place with blacktop or sidewalks. Give children squares of bubble wrap to lay on the sidewalk and stomp on. Enlist children in gathering up the popped wrap and putting it in a recycling bin.

Bible Emphasis

Note: A portable microphone may be needed for very large groups.

Gather everyone together and sing patriotic songs, such as "My Country 'Tis of Thee" and "O Beautiful for Spacious Skies," plus a few other favorites. Conclude the singing with "How Great Thou Art." Then call on the speaker for a brief message on the responsibility we have to use our political freedom to work toward the things of God, such as peace, justice, an end to poverty, and the sharing of the gospel of Christ (per Luke 12:49b, "And from everyone who has been given much, shall much be required"). The speaker may also want to talk about the freedom we have through faithfulness to God, based on Psalm 119:45: "I shall walk at liberty, for I have sought your precepts."

Barbecue and Dessert Contest

Supplies needed:

■ grills and other cookout supplies

■ camera and film (for photographing
entrants holding the desserts)

■ award ribbons

■ prizes (such as refrigerator magnets,
paper chef hats, funny mugs, or potholders)

Have a cookout with hot dogs and hamburgers, salads, and cold
drinks. Also consider hosting a parent/child dessert-making contest. Have contestants make the desserts at home and bring them
ready for serving at the event. Judge the contest early on, so people can enjoy the desserts. Make the award ceremony a highlight
of the picnic. If you do not plan to have a dessert contest, serve
cold watermelon for dessert.

▼ ▼ ▼ ▼ ▼ ▼ ▼ ▼ ▼ ▼ ▼ ▼ ▼ ▼ ▼ ▼ ▼ ▼

PARTY 7
Thanksgiving Party

GEARED FOR:
ADULTS AND FAMILIES

Prizes (pick one or two kinds, or have a variety set out for winners to choose from): candy, small calendars, calendar stickers, small pumpkin- or spice-scented candles, Thanksgiving- and Christmas-themed stickers, etc.

Do ahead:

■ Read "What Makes a Great Party?" on pages ix–xi.

■ Advertise the party, suggesting that people dress for the weather and bring a wrapped Thanksgiving holiday treat to present to a church family.

■ Plan in advance which individuals you will be visiting and prepare them for your visit, making sure they know that you won't need any refreshments or anything else that might be a hardship.

■ Decide how you will handle your schedule, since this is a party as well as an outing. (For example: It might be best to do the card making and the caroling in the same day, so that the groups go caroling while enthusiasm is still high, and in that case, decide to omit the game or play it with groups that finish early or while groups wait for the paint to dry; or you may decide to have refreshments before groups leave to carol; or it might be satisfying to regroup later to share stories and have refreshments.)

■ Ask appliance stores, furniture stores, or a contractor to save large, flat boxes for you—it may help to have friends help with this task.

■ Make sure each small group will include a person who will transport the card to the caroling sites.

■ Make a sample holiday card.

Welcome Table and Opening Activity
Supplies needed:

■ nametags

■ markers

■ pencils, one per guest

As people arrive, have each one find someone he or she doesn't know (or hasn't seen recently). The two people should share favorite Thanksgiving memories and share their plans for Thanksgiving dinner. If the hosts see someone with no one to talk to, they should introduce themselves and start a conversation.

Main Program: Singing Holiday Card
Supplies needed for each group:

■ copies of Thanksgiving songs or Christmas carols

■ large appliance-size boxes (preferably from a refrigerator, freezer, door, or unassembled furniture)

■ box cutters

■ poster paints and 2-inch or 4-inch brushes

■ hair dryers (to speed the paint drying process)

■ black markers with thick tips for making posters

- construction paper
- white glue sticks
- Thanksgiving or Christmas coloring pages from the Internet
- holiday decorations that can be taped, hot glued, or wired to the cards (bulletin decorations, wreaths, scarecrows, plastic pumpkins cut in half, corn stalks, holiday flowers, etc.) or purchase full door decorations to glue to the cardboard and have carolers use them as-is or use parts of them to create the inside of the card
- overhead projector (optional)
- transparencies on which people can trace pictures to project
- pencils
- floral wire

This could look like a big project to the guests attending your party. It will help if a sample is made and two or three carolers deliver the singing holiday card to the party group. When guests see how fun it can be, they will want to participate. Explain to your guests that you will be making giant holiday cards for people who need some encouragement. Review those you will be visiting and give a brief description of their situations (long-term family illness, recent loss, alone during the holidays, etc.) Further explain that you will caroling at the homes of these people when you deliver the cards and also will be sharing Thanksgiving treats. Review directions below and set guests to work.

1. Cut one of the big boxes to be a hinged greeting card. Make the card large enough that a few people can stand inside it when it is opened.

2. Make oval cutouts in the cover to allow your heads to poke through. (Be sure to make the holes the right height.)

▼ ▼ ▼ ▼ ▼ ▼ ▼ ▼ ▼ ▼ ▼ ▼ ▼ ▼ ▼ ▼ ▼ ▼

Incorporate the head holes in pictures of pilgrims, carolers, or a nativity scene, etc.

3. Make the outside of the card into a regular greeting card. Or cut out a huge rectangle on the inside of the card. When the card is opened, the rectangle will become the frame through which the group sings. Or you could stand inside the card and sing that way. To make the card designing go faster, offer groups a variety of Thanksgiving or Christmas coloring pages which can be enlarged on the card freehand or traced onto a transparency to project onto a card and traced that way.

Game: Pin the Head on the Turkey

Plan your party schedule before you prepare the game. It will help you decide how many sets of games you will need. If all the groups will play at the same time, you will need multiple sets. *Supplies needed:*

■ large cardboard turkeys, either made or purchased at a school-supply store (one per every 8–15 people)

■ cut-out photocopies of the turkey's head, one per person

■ tape or clay-like removable adhesive, such as Tak 'N Stik by Ross

■ blindfolds (two per team)

■ clear sticky adhesive paper to laminate the turkey and possibly the heads (optional)

Even adults, if led by an enthusiastic leader, will enjoy this variation of a children's game. To make photocopies of the turkey's head, cut off the cardboard turkey's head and copy it three or four times and then arrange them on a single paper so that you can make multiple copies at once. To allow you to use the game more than once, spread clear contact paper over both sides of the game pieces. Place a dab of removable adhesive or a rolled piece of tape on each head. Before the party, use tape or removable adhesive to put up the turkeys at locations in the room where teams can walk at least six feet to reach them. All the turkeys can be on one wall, as long as they are three or four feet apart.

To play the game, have guests line up in smaller groups, in front of a turkey. The groups are not competing against one another. Smaller groups will insure a shorter wait. Hand out the heads and ask each person to write his or her name on the head. (Transparency marker can be wiped off laminated heads later.) Explain that each person should try to stick the head on the turkey at the correct spot. To make it more difficult, spin the person around before pointing him or her toward the poster. While one person is going, the next person in line should put on the second blindfold. This will speed things up greatly. Give a prize to the person from each team who gets it closest to the correct spot.

Car Game: Stuff the Turkey
While the group is driving to the house or houses at which they will carol, here's a fun game they can play. One person says, "I stuffed my uncle's turkey with _____." The person finishes the statement with anything he or she desires. The passenger repeats the sentence and includes the previous suggestion, plus gives a new one. As it goes around the car, everyone must repeat each addition, in order, and add another. The first person to miss earns the letter *T*. That first person gets to try again the next round. The second person to miss earns the letters *T-U*. That second person gets to try again the next round. The first person to spell *T-U-R-K-E-Y* loses.

Bible Emphasis

■ copies of "Holiday Coupon" (page 42), several for each guest
■ list of people you will be visiting

Before groups go caroling, practice together a verse of each song they will sing. Say something like: *"We are Christ's hands and feet and voice on earth. Some of the people we will visit today are struggling with hard times. They might not have the energy to create their own Thanksgiving or Christmas. Our brief visit today may be something they think about for weeks!*

Some of you may want to do more. November and December are very busy for all of us and extra hard for those with special difficulties. You might consider filling out a coupon for something you can offer to ease the holidays for those you will visit. For example, you might offer a ride to the grocery store, help wrapping gifts, help decorating and undecorating, double a holiday recipe so they can have half of what you make, or extend an invitation to your home. Review the list of people you'll be visiting and spend some time in prayer. If you feel led to do so, fill out a coupon to give someone when you visit.

Make blank coupons available for people to fill in with their name, phone number, and what they want to offer. Encourage them to print in large letters as some of those you visit may have weak eyesight.

Refreshments

If you have planned that groups will return after caroling, you could serve hot cider and gingersnaps, gingerbread, or cake donuts. If you would like to serve a meal, try turkey sandwiches, cranberry gelatin salad, turkey-shaped cookies, and coffee, tea, punch, or cider.

Holiday Coupon

Given to: _____

From: _____

Good for: _____

_____

_____

Please call when you would like to redeem your coupon.

Phone Number: _____

Holiday Coupon

Given to: _____

From: _____

Good for:

_____

_____

Please call when you would like to redeem your coupon.

Phone Number: _____

PARTY 8
Gingerbread Christmas

This party during Advent combines the holiday tradition of making gingerbread houses with celebration of the Christ-child who was destined to "exalt the humble and fill the hungry with good things." If you prefer not to make three-dimensional gingerbread houses, consider baking large house-shaped cookies or cupcakes. You will need at least three per person so each participant has one to eat and two to share.

Having a group gingerbread party brings the cost down considerably because each family or individual can donate two or three kinds of candy. That way there will be plenty of variety of house toppings for everyone, and plenty of extra materials for making treats for others.

▼ ▼ ▼ ▼ ▼ ▼ ▼ ▼ ▼ ▼ ▼ ▼ ▼ ▼ ▼ ▼ ▼ ▼

Do Ahead:

■ Read "What Makes a Great Party?" on pages ix–xi.

■ Plan in advance which individuals will be recipients of the cards you will be signing and the treats you will be making.

■ If you've never made a gingerbread house, review how to do so from a library book or Web site.

■ Be sure to note on the invitation and the publicity materials that families and individuals must RSVP for the party. You'll need to know what items guests can donate to the party and how many supplies to have prepared ahead of time for the party. Mention also that you will be making treats to share with those who are shut-in or in need and ask for suggestions of persons who might appreciate receiving a treat or a card.

■ See how many families or individuals can bake their own gingerbread (or bring cookies or cupcakes, depending on the activity you choose). Or find bakers who will commit to baking gingerbread house sets (each house needs six pieces of gingerbread). Consider finding a person from your church or community who has experience making gingerbread houses and could be available to answer the little questions that arise before and during the party.

■ Provide a list of possible candy items and ask participants to bring some to the party. Have a sign-up sheet for candy so that you are sure to get a variety and some of the harder-to-find kinds and so that you can know which items you'll need to purchase. Here is a partial list of possibilities: candy canes of all sizes; sugar-frosted mini shredded wheat (for thatched roof); gumdrops; peppermints; candy swirl sticks; M&M's; Snow-Caps; Red Hots; silver dragees; nonpareils; colored sugars; Necco wafers; red and black licorice bites, ropes and twists; gum; Hershey's Chocolate Bars; miniature pretzels of all shapes; candy pebbles; chocolate chips; Lifesavers (can be melted and rehardened as window glass); wafer cookies; round swirled peppermints; ice-cream cones of all shapes and sizes (for the trees and turrets); sugar-coated almonds; jelly beans; Chiclets; candy orange sections; and root beer barrels.

■ Arrange the room so that two or three families or groups of individuals work at tables and have easy access to the candy.

■ Prepare undecorated extra gingerbread cookies and cupcakes ahead of time to give to others. (You'll decorate them during the party.)

Welcome Table and Opening Activity
Supplies needed:
■ nametags
■ markers
■ assorted Christmas cards and brightly-colored pens

Invite participants to gather together and share some of their favorite memories of Christmas. Remind them that for many people, Christmas is a difficult time and explain that you are going to make gingerbread houses (or decorate cookies or cupcakes) and sign cards to be given away. Review your list of suggestions and decide as a group who will be given cards, treats, or both, and match up the list of recipients with volunteers who will deliver the cards and treats. Lay out the cards and invite participants to sign each one and add a little message, if they wish.

Activity: Making Gingerbread Houses (or decorating cookies or cupcakes)
Supplies needed:
■ one gingerbread house (four walls and two roof pieces) for each family or individual (or gingerbread cookies or cupcakes if you choose to decorate those instead of making houses)

■ candy

■ bowls (for each candy variety so that guests can transport the candy to their tables)

■ royal icing, a candy glue with incredible holding power (one cup per family or individual)

■ resealable quart freezer bags (place one cup of royal icing in each one). When you snip off a tiny corner of the bag, tilt the bag, and squeeze the icing out through the snipped corner, the bag enables users to control the flow of icing.

■ scissors (for adult to snip end off icing bag)

■ plastic knives—if participants would prefer to smooth the icing rather than squeeze it out from the freezer bag

■ aluminum-foil-covered boards for the gingerbread houses to sit on. Be sure that each covered board is amply sized: there should be a four-inch border beyond the gingerbread house to allow for decorating the sides and bottom of the house. Participants might want to decorate a "walkway" around the house.

■ plastic wrap for transporting the completed houses, cookies, or cupcakes

Set people up with all the supplies needed and let them work at their own paces on the gingerbread houses or on decorating cookies or cupcakes. While they work, lead singing of Christmas carols with a creative way of taking requests, such as going in this order:

1. from someone whose birthday is in December

2. from someone who has made gingerbread houses before

3. from the youngest person present (or a family member who accompanies him or her)

4. from someone who does not send out Christmas cards

5. from someone who is wearing red

6. from someone who is going out of town on Christmas day

▼ ▼ ▼ ▼ ▼ ▼ ▼ ▼ ▼ ▼ ▼ ▼ ▼ ▼ ▼ ▼ ▼ ▼

7. from someone who has guests coming in for the holiday

After the houses, cookies, or cupcakes have been decorated, have people spend time walking around to enjoy all of the creations.

Bible Emphasis

Gather participants together and read aloud Mary's song from Luke 1:46-55. Make sure everyone is clear on the cards or treats they are delivering. Offer a prayer that the gifts would help others know God's love this Christmas.

Refreshments

It's difficult for children to see so much candy being used for decorating and not for eating, no matter how special the end product. Ask everyone to go to one of the prepared tables and to decorate extra cookies or cupcakes, both for others and to enjoy at the party. Also provide some finger sandwiches cut in shapes like a tree, a star, or a candy cane. Serve coffee, tea, milk or juice.

SECTION TWO

Small Group Parties

The purpose of the small group parties is to get members to the place that they can become friends outside of the class. Small group parties are good for youth groups, Sunday school classes, women's fellowships, men's organizations, deacons, singles' groups, prayer groups, Bible studies, and other separate entities in the church. A small group can usually meet in a home, where people can get acquainted more easily. Often the parties listed in this chapter would work, with a little adaptation, for any size group. However, these parties will require a more intimate atmosphere. If the small group parties are interspersed with other large group parties during the year, the small group becomes not a clique but an added blessing.

Such fellowship requires pre-planning:

■ Select several people to prepare and present the party, do the publicity, refreshments, games, set up and clean up, and devotions.

■ Set the date weeks in advance at a time that does not conflict with larger, all-church socials.

■ Send publicity out at least two weeks before the party date.

■ Select a home with a large family or living room.

■ Check a few days before the party to be sure everything is taken care of.

■ Since publicity is essential, find someone to call on expected guests as a reminder during the week preceding the party and to handle announcements in small group meetings.

PARTY 9
Hey, Who Are You?

GEARED FOR: ADULTS

Prizes (pick one or two kinds, or have a variety set out for winners to choose from): candy, luggage tags, emergency I.D. cards for wallets, bookmarks displaying the names of God, pocket-size address books from the dollar store, sets of party nametags

Do ahead:
■ Read "What Makes a Great Party?" on pages ix–xi.
■ Select the activities and prepare materials.
■ Ask guests to bring an appetizer or a dessert to share with others. Examples of easy-to-bring foods include chips and dip, vegetables and dip, breads, pies, and cookies.

Welcome Table and Opening Activity
Supplies needed:
■ nametags, with numbers only (see Opening Activity)
■ markers
■ one piece of paper per person
■ pencils, one per person

It's easy to be in a group for years with people you don't really know by name. As people arrive, ask them to wear a blank nametag, with only a number on it. Give each person a piece of paper and a pencil, and ask each person to put the numbers and the guests' full names (first, middle, and last names) on the sheet, encouraging them to talk to each guest. Each person must give his or her full name, including middle name, right off the bat to each person he or she meets. This will avoid embarrassing people who feel they should already know someone's name. After ten minutes, check to see if guests discovered all names correctly by having everyone share his or her name and hometown. Then guests write their full names on their nametags.

Game: Shadrach, Meshach, and Abednego

Ask everyone to sit in a circle. The leader can be "It" the first time. "It" points to someone in the circle and yells "Shadrach," "Meshach," or "Abednego." If "It" says "Shadrach," the person pointed at must tell the name of the person sitting to the left. If "It" says "Meshach," the person pointed at must give his or her own name. If "It" says "Abednego," the person pointed at must say the name of the person to the right. As soon as "It" says one of the names, "It" begins counting to ten as quickly as possible. If the person cannot come up with the right name before "It" reaches ten, the person becomes the new "It." Otherwise, "It" continues until someone falters and becomes the new "It."

Game: Name Quiz

Supplies needed:
- one piece of paper per person
- pencils, one per person

Hand out paper and pencils to the party guests. Read the following list and have guests record their answers on the paper. After you've gone through all 10 questions, share the answers and give a prize to the person(s) who got the most items correct.

Quiz:

1. Cary Grant's real name (Archibald Leach)

2. Name of U. S. senator from here (answers vary)

3. Name of the local mayor (answers vary, depending upon where guests reside)

4. Name of inventor of the cotton gin (Eli Whitney)

5. Name of a Civil War president (Jefferson Davis or Abraham Lincoln)

6. Name of vice president of the U.S.A. (varies each election year)

7. The apostle Paul's other name (Saul of Tarsus)

8. Name of a Bible prophet (any Old Testament prophet or John the Baptist)

9. Mark Twain's real name (Samuel Langhorne Clemens)

10. C. S. Lewis's full name (Clive Staples Lewis)

Game: The Toothpick Game

Supplies needed:

■ toothpicks, 20 per guest. (For large groups, substitute dried beans for toothpicks and give out more.)

■ something to catch the toothpicks (such as a towel)

Give each person twenty toothpicks for starters. Explain: *"The object of the game is to place a toothpick onto the towel [or whatever you use] every time you hear a statement that's true about you. The first person to get rid of all the toothpicks wins."* Then begin reading statements. Take time before the game to have people add items to the list, if you want to customize the list.

Throw in a toothpick if:

▪ you speak more than two languages

▪ you've ever fallen asleep in a ballpark during a game

- you've eaten sushi
- you've gotten into the wrong car in a parking lot
- you've never asked for an extension on your income tax
- you've been in a science fair
- you've finished reading more than one book this week
- you've read a poem this week
- you've taken a vitamin today
- you've played with a dog today
- you've ever forgotten a family member's birthday
- you've had more than three cups of coffee today
- you've gone scuba diving
- you've helped in the church nursery sometime this year
- you've ever washed diapers
- you've played a glockenspiel
- you've been to South America
- you've seen the same movie in a theater more than eight times
- you've danced the Macarena this year
- you've gone mountain climbing
- you've ever owned a pet turtle
- you've sewn a Halloween costume
- you've tipped a waiter more than thirty percent
- you've put catsup on eggs
- you've asked Santa for a horse
- you've maintained a composting bin
- you've coaxed a houseplant to grow
- you've been on television
- you've touched Plymouth Rock
- you've dived off a high dive
- you've sung in the shower this week
- you've taken a long-distance Amtrak trip
- you've flown a plane

- you've toasted a perfect marshmallow
- you've taught English to someone
- you've won a prize in an art contest
- you've sung in a church choir
- you've eaten Hawaiian poi
- you've skipped the turkey on Thanksgiving
- you're a short wave radio operator
- you've ever parachuted

Activity: A Name and a Calling
Supplies needed:
- baby name books
- computer with Internet access to search for *baby names,* "*Christian 'spiritual meaning of names,'*" etc. (optional)
- paper and pencils for each person

Explain: "*Throughout the Bible, people's names are significant. Names were used to note spiritual heritage, calling, and standing with God. For example, Anne (or Anna or Hannah) means 'grace,' and both Jonathan and Nathan mean 'gift of God.' Do you know why your parents chose your name? We are going to work with partners to come up with special meanings for our names. You can use a name book, if you want, or just come up with a definition that suits who you are.*" Pass out the baby name books and boot up the laptop if you have access to the Internet at your location.

Bible Emphasis
Sing some songs that praise the name of Jesus, such as "There Is a Name I Love to Hear," by Frederick Whitfield; "The Name of Jesus," words by W. C. Martin and music by E. S. Lorenz; and "Bless His Holy Name," by Andrae Crouch.

Finish with a short talk on the "I Ams," the names of Jesus in John's Gospel.

When Moses insisted that his people would want to know exactly who was calling them out of Egypt, God identified himself to Moses as "I AM WHO I AM." (Exodus 3:13-14). God gave this name because it expressed his character as dependable, capable, thoroughly trustworthy. Jesus used the same phrase of himself in John 8:58-59. He said, "Very truly, I tell you, before Abraham was, I am!" Discuss some of the ways in which Jesus clarified "I am":

"I am the good shepherd" John 10:14.

"I am the gate" John 10:9.

"I am the way, and the truth, and the life" John 14:6.

"I am the bread of life" John 6:35.

"I am the true vine" John 15:1.

"I am the Alpha and the Omega, the first and the last, the beginning and the end" Revelation 22:13.

"I am the resurrection and the life" John 11:25.

"I am the root and the descendent of David, the bright morning star" Revelation 22:16.

Refreshments

Have simple snacks such as cheese and crackers or veggies and dip on hand to make sure there's plenty. At the beginning of the party, set out the appetizers and desserts brought by the party guests. Serve soft drinks, juices, coffee, and tea.

PARTY 10
Football Party

GEARED FOR: MIXED GROUPS OR MEN'S GROUPS

Prizes (pick one or two kinds, or have a variety set out for winners to choose from): football cards, football key chains, football candy, football decals, football game schedules, tickets to a high-school football game

Do ahead:
- Read "What Makes a Great Party?" on pages ix–xi.
- Select activities, prepare materials, and plan refreshments.
- Come up with a list of people who are sports fans and could use some encouragement (adults, teens or children who are home-bound, ill, impoverished, or otherwise going through a hard time)

Welcome Table and Opening Activity
Supplies needed:
- used footballs or ones made from cardboard
- permanent markers, to sign footballs and nametags
- nametags
- labels with names of football recipients

Stick a label with the name of a recipient on each football. As people sign their nametags, have them also autograph several foot-

balls, adding a word of encouragement, if they like. Ask for volunteers and arrange to deliver the footballs later to the sports fans.

Game Football Match
Supplies needed:
- one piece of paper per person
- pencils, one per person

Pass out the paper and pencils and read the
names of football teams, asking party
guests to write down the name of each
team's city. For extra credit, have guests circle any teams they've seen play in person.

1. Giants (New York)
2. Redskins (Washington)
3. Eagles (Philadelphia)
4. Browns (Cleveland)
5. Cowboys (Dallas)
6. Bears (Chicago)

7. Dolphins (Miami)
8. Patriots (New England)
9. Lions (Detroit)
10. Raiders (Oakland)
11. 49ers (San Francisco)
12. Steelers (Pittsburgh)

Game: Football Throw
Supplies needed:
- sponge football
- appliance box or other large box

Cut 4 holes into the big carton. Under each hole print the scores: 6
points, 7 points, 3 points, 1 point. Divide the people into two teams.
Place the box about 15 feet from the line of people. Have team
members, one at a time, toss the ball at the carton and try to get it
into one of the holes. Keep score. Each winner receives a prize.

Game: Football Games

Supplies needed:
- electronic or manual football games
- recorded great/classic games, television, VCR or DVD player

Place electric or manual football games around a room. Let guests go to one of the games and play. Divide the guests according to the number of games you borrowed. Others can watch old, favorite games. This activity can last for 20 to 30 minutes.

Game: Charades

Supplies needed:
- pads and pencils, for those who decide to sketch clues rather than act them out
- names of football teams, cut apart and placed in paper bag
- minute timer

Write the following teams on slips of paper and place in a paper bag:

Buffalo Bills; Baltimore Ravens; Houston Texans; Denver Broncos; Miami Dolphins; Cincinnati Bengals; Indianapolis Colts; Kansas City Chiefs; New England Patriots; Cleveland Browns; Jacksonville Jaguars; Oakland Raiders; New York Jets; Pittsburgh Steelers; Tennessee Titans; San Diego Chargers; Dallas Cowboys; Chicago Bears; Atlanta Falcons; Arizona Cardinals; New York Giants; Detroit Lions; Carolina Panthers; Saint Louis Rams; Philadelphia Eagles; Green Bay Packers; New Orleans Saints; San Francisco 49ers; Washington Redskins; Minnesota Vikings; Tampa Bay Buccaneers; and Seattle Seahawks.

Divide the group into two teams. Say: *"We're going to play sports charades. You can act out or draw clues. One team will send up a player who pulls a paper from the bag and has 60 seconds to get his team to guess the football team listed on the paper. If the player is successful, the team gets a point. Play alternates between teams. The game ends when all team names have been used.*" Award prizes to winners.

Game: Instant Replay
Supplies needed:
- paper, one piece per person
- pencils, one for each person

Give everyone a paper and pencil and at the count of three, ask the guests to write down as many professional football teams as they can remember in four minutes. When the time is up, ask the guests to count up their lists. The one with the most teams reads his or her list aloud. Distribute prizes to those with the highest scores.

Bible Emphasis
Ask a former football player, coach, or enthusiast to share a short message comparing and contrasting a football game to the Christian life. You could also do a search on the Internet or at the library for articles on football players who are active Christians. Read together Philippians 3:14 and sing favorite gospel choruses.

Refreshments
Serve foot-long sandwiches or ballpark food and soft drinks or have a sheet cake with a football frosted onto the top with coffee, tea, or milk.

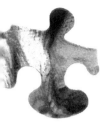

PARTY 11
Puzzles Galore

GEARED FOR: ADULTS

Prizes for this party could include: giant cookies cut (while warm) into jigsaw-puzzle shapes, candy, erasable pens (for crossword puzzles), crossword puzzles, and small jigsaw puzzles.

Do ahead:
■ Read "What Makes a Great Party?" on pages ix–xi.
■ Select activities, prepare materials, and plan refreshments.
■ Prepare the nametags (without guests' names on them) ahead of time. (See the Welcome Table for instructions.)

Welcome Table and Opening Activity
Supplies needed:
■ nametags
■ markers
■ rubber stamps and ink pads
■ paperclips

Stamp something special on the nametags. Cut nametags into puzzle pieces, making sure each piece has an outside edge. Gather the pieces of each tag together and paperclip them together. As guests arrive, have each put a nametag puzzle together, print his or her name on it, and put it on.

Game: Missing Link
Supplies needed:
- 3 cardboard puzzles made for small children (8–12 large pieces)
- 3 tables, each with 1 puzzle piece

Give everyone two or three pieces of a puzzle. Guests add their pieces to the single pieces on the tables to complete the puzzles. Whoever completes a puzzle with one of his or her pieces, receives a prize.

Game: Puzzle Race
Supplies needed:
- calendar pictures, one picture per person
- scissors, one pair per person
- paperclips

Give everyone a picture from an old calendar. Provide scissors, and have each guest cut the picture in ten pieces and clip the pieces together. Place the clipped-and-gathered puzzle pieces on tables. At the count of three, everyone goes to a table, takes someone else's puzzle, and puts it together. The first person finished gets a prize.

Game: Puzzling Quiz
Supplies needed:
- stack of play money (from board games)
- Trivial Pursuit (optional)

Shuffle the play money so that the denominations are interspersed within in the pile.

Players will earn money by answering questions (use those below or from Trivial Pursuit). You can do this by sitting everyone in a circle and giving each person a question, one at a time. Or you can have three special chairs for three contestants at a time, each of which will answer three rounds of questions. Each correct answer is worth whatever bill is on top of the stack of money. If interest is great enough, go around at least three times. The person with the highest dollar amount in the end receives a prize.

Puzzling Questions:
- How do you spell *Chicago*?
- How do you spell *Minneapolis*?
- What state is north of California? (Oregon)
- What state is north of New Mexico? (Colorado)
- What state is north of Alabama? (Tennessee)
- Who became president after George Washington? (John Adams)
- Who became president after Franklin D. Roosevelt? (Harry Truman)
- Who became president after Richard Nixon? (Gerald Ford)
- What ocean is east of the United States? (Atlantic)
- What ocean is east of Hawaii? (Pacific)
- What ocean is south of Australia? (Indian)
- Who wrote "Romeo and Juliet"? (William Shakespeare)
- Who wrote "The Messiah"? (George Freidrich Handel)
- Who wrote "The Raven"? (Edgar Allen Poe)
- Who gave the speech "Ain't I a Woman?" (Sojourner Truth)
- Who wrote "Amazing Grace"? (John Newton)
- Who was famous for singing "God Bless America"? (Kate Smith)
- Multiply 9 x 6 (54)

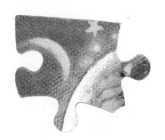

- Multiply 8 x 4 (32)
- Multiply 11 x 7 (77)

Game: Puzzling Words
Supplies needed:
- paper, one sheet per person
- pencil, one for each person

Hand out paper and pencils then quickly read the following scrambled letters. Give guests a few minutes to unscramble the words. The first person to unscramble all the words receives a prize.
Puzzling Words:

1. u   p   z   l   z   e   (puzzle)

2. r   t   y   a   p   (party)

3. u   t   l   r   a   h   e   g   (laughter)

4. c   c   r   h   h   u   (church)

5. g   e   m   a   s   (games)

6. h   s   e   r   e   f   r   m   n   t   e   s   (refreshments)

7. p   y   p   a   h   (happy)

8. o   f   e   f   e   c   (coffee)

9. e   x   l   a   r   (relax)

10. e   e   l   w   m   c   o   (welcome)

Bible Emphasis

Begin by singing songs of faith, such as: "Tell Me Why the Stars Do Shine" and "I Don't Know Why," and end with "It Is No Secret What God Can Do," by Stuart Hamblen, changing the word *secret* to *puzzle*.

Review some examples from Matthew's gospel of how Jesus' opponents tried to use puzzling questions to discredit him:

■ Matthew 22:36: Which commandment in the law is the greatest?   *37*

■ Matthew 22:17: Is it lawful to pay taxes to the emperor, or not?"

■ Matthew 22:28: In the resurrection, then, whose wife of the seven will she be?"

And then, read in Matthew 21:23-37 and in Luke 10:25-37 how Jesus used questions to thwart those who challenged him.

Discuss what we can learn from Jesus' approach to his opponents.

Refreshments

Have sandwiches and chips or salads. End up with a large sheet cake that looks like a jigsaw puzzle or is decorated with a question mark. For drinks, make a punch that's a mixture of different juices or different soft drinks. Write the contents on a card left upside down. See who can guess the contents of the punch.

PARTY 12
Fun with Nature

GEARED FOR: ADULTS

Prizes (pick one or two kinds, or have a variety set out for winners to choose from): seed packets, small plants, plant markers, bags of Animal Crackers

Do ahead:
- Read "What Makes a Great Party?" on pages ix–xi.
- Select activities, prepare materials, and plan refreshments.
- Be on the lookout for T-shirt sales and get the word out to others to watch out for sales. If necessary, ask each guest to bring a white T-shirt to decorate.

Welcome Table and Opening Game
Supplies needed:
- nametags
- markers
- pencils, one per person
- copy of "How Does Your Garden Grow?" (page 68) for each person (enlarge when photocopying)

Give everyone a game sheet, and ask guests to get as many signatures as they can. Each person may sign as many sheets as he or she wishes, but each guest can only sign a person's sheet in three spaces. Explain that there will be two winners: the person who gets the most spaces signed and the one who gets the most signatures for a single category.

After about eight minutes, gather guests and award prizes to each winner. As the group sits around a circle, encourage discussion with questions such as: *"Who gardens for a hobby? What are people's favorite garden stores or outdoor activities? Who is the most creative gardener (adapting to apartment living, for example)? What vegetables do people can or freeze?*

HOW DOES YOUR GARDEN GROW?

favorite flower is rose

grows organic produce

has a vegetable garden

saves castoff flower or vegetable pots

visits a garden center at least six times a summer

grows watermelons

prefers the company of animals

cans own tomatoes or other vegetables

talks to houseplants

composts

does creative gardening (e.g. square foot, in pots, indoors)

enjoys an outdoor activity (list it)

is a non-gardener married to a gardener (vice versa)

has grown roots in the refrigerator veggie bin

has five or more flower catalogs at home

Activity: Painting T-shirts

Supplies needed for up to twenty guests:

■ white T-shirts, one per person as well as a few for samples
■ fabric paint: four ounces each; 8 different, complementary colors
■ drop cloths, newspaper, or discarded plastic table cloths
■ eight clean spray bottles—bottles with adjustable nozzles work best
■ leaves, fronds, ferns (artificial greenery as an alternative and if woods are nearby, guests can collect their own)
■ plastic bags (two per shirt)
■ paper towels and baby wipes or cloth rags
■ T-shirt directions to display (optional)

Preparation:

1. Prepare sprayers by emptying each color of fabric paint into a clean sprayer and adding 1½ cups of water to the spray bottle, then screwing the top on and shaking vigorously. Experiment by spraying a rag or paper towel to set the sprayer on a fine spray.
2. Create a sample shirt following the directions below.
3. Spread out drop cloths on floor and tables.
4. Print out directions below on newsprint or type up several copies if you think your guests will need them.

Directions:

1. Gather a variety of leaves.
2. Line the inside of a blank, white shirt with a plastic grocery bag and turn it on its back on the drop cloth.
3. Select paints, taking care not to choose colors that become muddy when combined.
4. Spread open the sleeves to spray them first, placing a leaf or two on the sleeve before spraying, if you want.

5. Arrange the leaves on the shirt and spray over them with different colors of paint, using a light mist. The mist around a leaf must hit the edges of the leaf to make the outline distinct. It's sometimes possible to nudge the drops of paint collecting on the leaf toward the edge so that the edges are defined. Try not to spray so many colors in one place that the paints turn into brown.

6. Remove leaves and repeat on the other side.

7. If the patterns turn out dark enough, it is sometimes possible to lightly mist a bit of very light color into the blank space when the leaves are removed, but too much over-spraying will eradicate the image.

8. In a short while the shirt will be dry enough to place into a clean plastic bag to bring home. At home, lay the shirt flat to dry completely. Delay washing it for at least 24 hours.

Game: Flower Mix Up

Supplies needed:

■ paper, one sheet per person
■ pencil, one for each person

Hand out paper and pencils and read off the scrambled letters below. Give guests a few minutes to unscramble the words. The first person to unscramble all the words receives a prize.

1. s y p n a   (pansy)
2. l l y i   (lily)
3. s r t a e   (aster)
4. d y i s a   (daisy)
5. o s r e   (rose)
6. r a a g d n e i   (gardenia)
7. d o c i r h   (orchid)
8. r o c c s u   (crocus)

9. p h d i u m e i n l   (delphinium)
10. f a f d i o l d   (daffodil)

Game: Animal Charades
Supplies needed:
■ names of animals on slips of paper (one animal per slip, see suggestions below)
■ paper bag or gift bag with animals on it
■ one-minute timer

Place the slips of paper with animal names in the paper bag. Divide the group into two teams. Alternating, each group sends someone to act out the animal name drawn from the bag, using sounds, actions, and descriptions, such as "I live in the ocean" or "I like to eat bamboo." Start the timer once the name is drawn. If the group guesses the name, the person can pull a new slip and act on another. If the group does not guess the animal, the slip goes back in the bag and play passes to the second team. One point is awarded to the team for each correct guess. Play ends when all animals have been guessed. Each person on the winning team chooses a prize. (Suggested animals: elephant, coyote, hyena, giraffe, cat, cow, donkey, dolphin, rabbit, panther, aardvark, fox, alpaca, caribou, cheetah, gazelle, goat, llama, koala, mouse, hamster, hippopotamus, otter, platypus, gopher, sheep, skunk, tiger, wart hog, zebra, wolf, octopus, kangaroo, panda, buffalo, alpaca, armadillo, beaver, bear, raccoon, jaguar, frog, turtle, cobra, alligator, chameleon, dragon, gorilla, and crocodile.

Game: Animal Quest
Supplies needed
■ Bibles without concordances

Divide guests into groups of three or four. Give each group a Bible. At the signal, call an animal name for the groups to find in the Bible. When found, the group yells: "Quest success!" and reads the verse aloud. Keep score to determine the winning team. Then the leader calls out another animal to locate in the Bible. If necessary, give a hint of one Bible book or chapter that mentions it. Cites are given below for each animal; however, all appear in many more texts.

- eagle (Exodus 19:4; Jeremiah 48:40)
- ewe (Genesis 21:29; 2 Samuel 12:6)
- horse (Hosea 14:3; Psalm 147:10)
- cattle (Exodus 12:38; Psalm 50:10)
- lion (Isaiah 11:6; Judges 14:6)
- ox (Job 6:5; 1 Timothy 5:18)
- donkey (Exodus 23:12; Matthew 21:5)
- wolf (Isaiah 11:6/64:25; Luke 10:3)

Bible Emphasis

Sing several songs about God's creation, such as "This Is My Father's World," "All Creatures of Our God and King," and "How Great Thou Art." For a devotional, choose one of the following options:

1. Review together the texts below and discuss the implications of God having relationship with animals and animals serving God's purposes.

- Balaam's donkey (Numbers 22:28-31)
- Elijah and the ravens (1 Kings 17:7-6)
- Jonah rescued by a fish (Jonah 2:1)

2. Have a Christian master gardener, wildlife expert, or nature center speaker share some thoughts on God's charge for us to care for his creation.

Refreshments

Serve refreshments that celebrate creation's natural bounty, such as fresh vegetables, fruit, teas, and juices. For more substantial fare, consider a potluck of salads, home-made soups, and home-made breads. Cupcakes decorated with flowers also are in keeping with the theme.

PARTY 13
Laugh a Lot

GEARED FOR: MIDDLE-SCHOOL GROUPS AND JUNIOR-HIGH GROUPS

Prizes (pick one or two kinds, or have a variety set out for winners to choose from): pins from a party store saying "World's Best Joke Teller," tricks from a joke shop, candy, or White Elephant gifts wrapped in Sunday comics

Do ahead:
■ Read "What Makes a Great Party?" on pages ix–xi.
■ Select the activities, prepare materials, and plan refreshments.

Welcome Table and Opening Activity

Supplies needed:
- nametags
- markers
- books with appropriate jokes
- copies of jokes, a different joke for each guest

As people arrive, hand each one a copy of a joke. Ask each guest to share the joke with at least three other people. If you cannot find enough jokes for each person to have a different one, give the same jokes to three people (without telling them who else has the joke) and have them find each other.

Game: Laugh Away

Supplies needed:
- bell
- 10 jokes, written on slips of paper or a good joke book

Gather the people together into a circle of chairs. Pass out jokes or pass a joke book from teller to teller. Tell guests they should laugh when they hear the bell ring and keep it up until the bell rings again. Have a practice round. Then tell a joke. Ring the beginning bell. Everyone should laugh. When the laughter begins to die down, ring the ending bell. From those who laughed the longest (or loudest), choose the person to tell the next joke. Continue the joke telling for about five or eight minutes or until six or eight people get to tell jokes.

Game: Tell Me Another

Ask for volunteers. Let everyone tell a favorite joke. It would be wise to prepare several guests ahead of time to avoid wasted time and any embarrassing jokes. The person voted best joke-teller wins a prize.

Game: Riddles

Supplies needed:
- lists of riddle questions, one per half the group
- lists of riddle answers, one per half the group
- paper, one piece per person
- pencil, one for each person

Give half the guests a list of all of the riddles and the other half a list of all of the answers. Guests need to pair with a partner and try to match up the questions and answers correctly. Allow about four minutes and then have different ones read the riddle and the correct answer. Those who get them all right can get a small prize. Answers are: 1d; 2f; 3g; 4a; 5c; 6h; 7b; 8e

Riddle questions:

1. What is black and white and read all over?

2. What has four wheels and flies?

3. What has four "eyes" but can't see?

4. What is the difference between a china shop and a furniture store?

5. What is air?

6. What is the fastest way to learn to be a barber?

7. Where did Martha Washington go after her thirty-ninth year?

8. Why did the turtle cross the road?

Riddle answers:

a. one sells tea sets and the other, settees

b. into her fortieth

c. a balloon with its skin removed

d. a newspaper

T *why do we be quiet in church (people are sleeping*

e. to get to the other side
f. a garbage truck
g. Mississippi
h. study all the short cuts

Game 5: Make It Up

Divide the guests into four groups. Ask them to make up an original joke or two. After about five minutes, bring the people back together and let one person from each group tell the new joke or jokes.

Bible Emphasis

Sing a few "happy" songs, such as "If You're Happy and You Know It," and close with "Happiness Is the Lord."

Share Proverbs 17:22 (A cheerful heart is a good medicine) and emphasize that God created us with the ability to laugh. Invite discussion of things that make us laugh. Discuss what kind of humor is appropriate for Christians. Note that much popular humor comes at someone's expense and that kind of humor is hurtful and therefore, not appropriate. Develop together a guideline for judging humor based on Philippians 4:8, "Whatever is true, whatever is commendable, if there is an excellence and if there is anything worthy of praise, think about these things."

Refreshments

Serve fun treats, such as ice cream sundaes, or "Moose Lips" (apple slices with peanut butter in between), or a cake with a smiley face.

PARTY 14
Thrills without Spills Meet

GEARED FOR: HIGH SCHOOL GROUPS AND COLLEGE GROUPS

Prizes: choose sports related items, such as tennis balls, sports whistles, wrist bands, foam footballs, and individual sports drinks.

Do ahead:
- Read "What Makes a Great Party?" on pages ix–xi.
- Select activities, prepare materials, and plan refreshments.

Welcome Table and Opening Activity

Supplies needed:

- nametags
- markers

Send guests on a "chase" to find a person who:

1. has run a marathon

2. is/was on a high school basketball team

3. watches the Olympics

4. would like to be a coach someday

Main Activity: Assorted Games

Note: If the party is planned outdoors with many guests, consider having games going on simultaneously at different locations.

Supplies needed:

- cones to mark marathon route
- stopwatch or timer
- extra large plastic ball
- balloons
- plastic hoop or rope
- foam discus or 8-inch circle cut from spongy material or Styrofoam

■ *Broad Jump:* Divide the guests into two teams. Draw a line on the floor or in the dirt, if you are gathering outside. Have the teams line up behind the line. One by one, each team member, jumps, with feet together. The team that has the longest jumps is the winner and each team member gets an award.

■ *Baby Steps Marathon:* Mark a course to run. Line up the two teams and explain that the marathon is to be "run" with baby steps, landing flat on the foot with each step. Let one person from each team race at a time, timing each participant from start to finish. Give a prize to the individuals with the lowest times. Then add the whole team scores together to find the winning team. As an alternative, if space allows, you may opt to run the marathon with everyone at once and, rather than timing the runs, give prizes to those who come in first, second, and third.

■ *Balloon Relay:* Divide into three teams. Have the teams line up with half the members on one side of the room (or outdoor space) and the other half a distance away. The relay is run while batting a balloon, keeping it up in the air the entire distance, then batting it to the next runner, who is waiting across the way. If the balloon drops, the runner goes back and starts over.

■ *Discus Throw:* Using a circular piece of foam as a discus, guests compete to throw the furthest distance.

■ *Team Play:* Instead of competing, in this activity, guests work together to reach the goal. Lay out the plastic hoop or create a circle with rope. At a distance of about ten feet away, gather guests into a seated circle. Place a large ball in the center of the circle. Explain that their job is to work together to get the ball into the hoop, but they can't use their hands. The game ends when the ball is placed in the hoop. Everyone wins.

Bible Emphasis
Sing songs about the Christian life such as "Pass it On" and "Seek Ye First." Discuss the Christian life as a race, referring to 1 Corinthians 9:25-26. Focus on the idea that both the goal and the prize of the race are faithfulness to God.

Refreshments
Serve pizza and sports drinks. Write numbers on strips of paper and place them in a basket. Toss the numbers from the basket into the air. Have each guest find a number. Start the refreshment line with the high-est number and work down.

PARTY 15
Teddy Bear Party

GEARED FOR: CHILDREN, AGES 5 TO 8

Prizes (rather than awarding prizes to winners, allow each child to select a prize at the end of the party—all are winners): baggies of teddy bear graham crackers, candy bears, and teddy bear stickers or miniature teddy bears

Do ahead:
■ Read "What Makes a Great Party?" on pages ix–xi.
■ Select activities, prepare materials, and plan refreshments.
■ Cut bowties from construction paper for each guest.
■ Gather many teddy bears of various sizes, shapes, and colors. If possible, include ones with glasses, hearing aids, or in a wheel chair.

Welcome Table and Opening Activity
Supplies needed:
■ nametags, one per guest, leader, and teddy bear
■ markers

■ teddy bear coloring pages from coloring books or the Internet
■ crayons or markers

As children arrive, provide lots of crayons or markers and pictures to color. Display completed pictures on the wall or on the backs of chairs.

Activity: Tiny Teddy Find
Supplies needed:
■ envelopes for collecting the tiny bears, one per child
■ teddy bear stickers affixed to small pieces of cardboard (for younger guests) or teddy bear confetti (for older children)

Before anyone arrives, hide teddy bear stickers or confetti around the room. When all the guests have gathered, explain that there are teddy bears hiding around the room. Show a sample of what you've hidden. Count to three and send the children off to find the hidden bears.

Game: Hidden T. B.
Supplies needed:
■ teddy bear suitable for hiding
■ familiar children's song

Carefully explain how to play the game, and sing a practice round of the song. Ask someone to be "It" and leave the room. Select one child to hide the teddy bear with part of the bear showing. When "It" comes back to find the teddy bear, the group sings a familiar song to guide the person searching. They sing quietly when "It" is far from the teddy bear and louder as he or she gets nearer to the bear. When "It" finds the teddy bear, the child who hid the bear becomes "It" and goes out. Continue until all have had a chance to both hide and find. The first person to be "It" should be the last to hide the bear.

Activity: Pin the Tie on the Teddy Bear
Supplies needed:
- a large picture of a teddy bear (poster or drawn), laminated if you wish
- tape or removable clay adhesive
- construction-paper bowtie for each child
- marker
- two blindfolds

Write each player's name on a separate bow tie. Place a rolled piece of tape or a pinch of clay adhesive on the back of the bowties. Explain that the game is like "Pin the Tail on the Donkey," but here, the goal is to place a bowtie on the neck of the bear. One at a time, give each child a turn by blindfolding him or her

and gently spinning the child once. To save time, blindfold the second child while the first child is taking a turn.

Activity: Teddy Bear Guessing Game

Supplies needed:

■ a large teddy bear, which you have named
■ an envelope with the bear's name written inside
■ list of clues to the bear's name in order of difficulty

Bring out the big teddy bear and explain that each child will try to guess the bear's name. (Use a name they wouldn't think of immediately.) Give the most difficult clue first, then move down the list, allowing guesses after each clue. If no child guesses correctly, open the envelope and show the correct name.

Sample Hints for the Name "Blueberry":

1. My bear is named after a yummy food.
2. This food ripens in the summer.
3. Wild bears like to eat this food.
4. I like to eat this food in pancakes.
5. My bear's name starts with the letter *B*.
6. There's a book about a girl named Sal who gathered this food in a little pail.
7. Sal met a bear who liked this food.
8. When I eat this food, my tongue turns blue.
9. The name of my bear is a kind of berry.
10. The name of my bear ends in the letter y.

Activity: Grizzly Bear, Grizzly Bear, Teddy Bear

This game is similar to "Duck, Duck, Goose," however, it is non-competitive. The children stand in a circle while "It" marches around the outside of the circle. "It" touches each person on the shoulder and says, "Grizzly Bear" until he or she chooses "Teddy Bear." The child tapped as "Teddy Bear" runs around the circle and back to his or her spot. "Teddy Bear" becomes "It" and the game continues. Each person may be tapped as "Teddy Bear" only once, so all are included. The drama of the last "Teddy Bear" comes down to when he or she will be tapped because "It" can continue around the circle more than once before calling out "Teddy Bear."

Bible Emphasis

Display the group of varied teddy bears. Talk about how each one is different and stress that it is the differences that make them special. Explain that God made each one of us special. Lead the group in reciting three times, "I am special because God made me."

Refreshments

Be sure to have healthy snacks for children who do not eat sugar. Snacks could include teddy bear cookies or "wild" fruit and vegetable pieces for children to "forage."

Large Group Parties

While large group par-
ties require larger meet-
ing spaces and more
planning, refreshments,
props, and committee
members than do small
group parties, the extra
effort can be worthwhile. Larger
groups can make guests feel more
comfortable trying activities and
sometimes people who attend alone feel
more comfortable in a sizeable crowd. A
church-wide social can offer increased
enjoyment, build lasting friendships,
and provide greater ministry opportuni-
ties—all things that make for a stronger
church fellowship.

When planning a large group party, it is a good idea to ask several enthusiastic people to take charge. Select game leaders, speakers, refreshment makers and servers, set-up and clean-up helpers, and people to prepare game props. It is also essential that *everyone* be invited to a large-group gathering, so no one feels left out. To help accomplish this mass invitation enlist a telephone squad, place several posters around the church, have parties listed in Sunday bulletins at least three weeks in advance, and make announcements in adult classes.

Be sure that each party is well-planned, that it progresses at a rapid pace, and that all details are attended to before the beginning of the event. A well-planned occasion, a well-organized event, and a happy gathering will make the party successful.

And, as always, be sure to back up the party with prayer.

PARTY 16
Balls, Balls, and More Balls (Sports Night)

GEARED FOR: YOUTH

Prizes (pick one or two kinds, or have a variety set out for winners to choose from): gum balls, malted milk balls, tiny Super Balls and other balls that come in value packs or as party favors.

Do ahead:
■ Read "What Makes a Great Party?" on pages ix–xi.
■ Select activities, prepare materials, and plan refreshments.

Welcome Table and Opening Activity
Supplies needed:
■ nametags (shaped like a ball)
■ markers
■ dozens of small balls (high-bounce balls)
■ bell or whistle

This is a great opportunity to have fun, fellowship, and share the gospel with newcomers and visitors. Since youth can be uncomfortable with adults they don't know, it might be helpful to have youth serve as greeters at the welcome table.

Before anyone arrives, hide small balls around the room. As guests arrive, ask them to put on nametags and then hunt for the balls. Ring a bell or blow a whistle to gather everyone together. Count balls and give a prize to the winner.

Game: Super Ball Bounce
Supplies needed:
- 12 small high-bounce balls

Hand out balls to a dozen guests. Those with the balls stand in the center of the circle and see who can bounce the balls the highest. The highest bouncer continues to compete as the balls are passed on to others. Continue until one person emerges as the champion and receives a prize.

Game: Pass
Supplies needed:
- tennis balls in two different colors
(two of each color for every 20–30 people)
- music you can start and stop

Have everyone sit in a large circle, preferably sitting on the floor, but chairs can be used if players sit close together. For large groups, make two concentric circles. Hand out four balls for every 20–30 people in a circle. Hold up one color ball and explain that this color ball gets passed (not thrown) to the right. Hold up the other color ball and explain that that color ball gets passed to the left. At the sound of music, the balls begin getting passed. Whoever has a ball when the music stops receives a penalty (see below). Keep the game going for about 10 minutes.

Possible penalities:

- sing a nursery rhyme
- stand on one foot for 60 seconds
- recite the alphabet backwards
- skip around the circle
- name ten animals
- walk 8 steps on all fours
- whistle a tune
- tell a joke

Game: Target Ball

Do ahead:

■ Use masking tape or chalk to draw circles on the floor for targets, printing a large (1000, 2000) point number inside each.

■ Mark a starting line with tape or chalk.

Supplies needed:

■ a net that can be put up quickly

■ balls

Put up the net and place the guests behind the starting line. Divide the group into two to four teams. Each team selects a scorekeeper. The teams take turns, allowing each person to throw a ball over the net at the targets, trying to get it to bounce in one of the score sections. Points are recorded. Continue until all have thrown once or twice. The winners go first in the refreshment line.

Game: Kickball
Supplies needed:
- sponge ball or beach ball the size of a kickball or volleyball
- baseball diamond marked on floor

Divide the group into two teams. If there are too many guests for two teams, have a second game going in another section of the building. Those who prefer not to play can serve as cheerleaders, umpires, and score keepers. Played like outdoor kickball, runners kick and run the bases. They can be tagged out when they are off a base. To abbreviate the game, you can have two outs per side. Play at least until all have had a chance to kick. For a noncompetitive alternative, allow each person a chance to kick and run the bases and each person a chance to pitch.

Bible Emphasis: Bible Baseball
Supplies needed:
- chairs for pitcher, first, second, and third bases, and home plate
- Bible with concordance (to check answers, if necessary)

Set up the "diamond" using chairs. Divide the group into two teams. As each player comes "up to bat," he or she chooses a difficulty category (single, double, triple, or home run) and the pitcher (a leader who is not on either team) asks the question and calls the answer a "hit" (correct) or an "out" (incorrect). Players advance bases accordingly and switch sides after three outs.

Singles:
1. Who was the first man? (Adam)
2. What did God do on the seventh day of creation? (rest)
3. Who swallowed Jonah? (a big fish)
4. Name one of the Ten Commandments (see Exodus 20)
5. Who built the ark? (Noah)
6. Who was the first woman? (Eve)

7. What did Delilah do to Samson's hair? (cut it)

8. Who was thrown into a den of lions? (Daniel)

9. In how many days did God create the world? (six)

10. What happened three days after Jesus died? (He arose.)

11. What is the last book of the Bible? (Revelation)

12. Who was Jesus' mother? (Mary)

13. Where was Jesus born? a stable or Bethlehem)

14. What is the first book in the Bible? (Genesis)

15. Who baptized Jesus? (John the Baptist)

Doubles:

1. Who led the slaves out of Egypt? (Moses)

2. Who is the oldest man in the Bible? (Methuselah)

3. Psalm 23 says, "The Lord is my _____." (shepherd)

4. What two parts is the Bible divided into? (Old and New Testaments)

5. Who had a coat of many colors? (Joseph)

6. Name two apostles (see Matthew 10:2-4)

7. Name all four Gospels. (Matthew, Mark, Luke, John)

8. What city's walls tumbled down when Joshua marched around it? (Jericho)

9. How many times did Peter deny Jesus? (three)

10. How many books are there in the Bible? (66)

11. Quote any verse from the Bible.

12. How many days did it rain in the Noah story? (40)

13. Who received the Ten Commandments? (Moses)

14. What book comes after Psalms? (Proverbs)

15. What did John the Baptist eat? (locusts and wild honey)

Triples:

1. Where did Jesus perform his first miracle? (Cana or a wedding)

2. Recite John 3:16. (See the Bible.)

3. Who came to Jesus at night? (Nicodemus)

4. Name one Old Testament prophet that begins with I, M, or Z. (Isaiah, Micah, Malachi, Zephaniah, or Zechariah)

5. Name a New Testament book that is not one of Gospels.

6. Name a Bible book that is named for a woman. (Esther or Ruth)

7. What did Jesus tell us to do to our enemies? (Love them.)

8. Who was Moses' brother? (Aaron)

9. What is the longest book in the Bible? (Psalms)

10. Who was the friend of Shadrach and Meshach? (Abednego)

11. Who was knocked to the ground by a bright light on his way to arrest Christians? (Saul or Paul)

12. What is the last book of the Old Testament? (Malachi)

13. What was Jesus' first miracle? (water into wine)

14. Who were the first people to visit the baby Jesus? (shepherds)

15. Who did Mary visit after she found out she was going to have a baby? (Elizabeth)

Home runs:

  1. Who was Isaac's father? (Abraham)

  2. Name a fruit of the Spirit (See Galatians 5:22.)

  3. What New Testament book tells the story of the early church? (Acts)

  4. Where was Jesus baptized? (The River Jordan)

  5. Who did Jesus raise from the dead? (Lazarus or little girl)

  6. Who were the first twins? (Jacob and Esau)

  7. Where did Moses receive the Ten Commandments? (Mt. Sinai)

  8. Which king built the first temple? (King Solomon)

  9. Recite one of the Beatitudes. (See Matthew 5:3-10.)

  10. Who was king of Israel before David? (Saul)

  11. Who was Moses' sister? (Miriam)

  12. Who saw the handwriting on the wall? (Nebuchadnezzar)

  13. What did Jesus celebrate in Jerusalem ate age 12? (Passover)

  14. Where did Noah's ark land? (Mt. Ararat)

  15. Where did Jesus grow up? (Nazareth)

Refreshments

Serve cakes shaped like footballs, softballs, or soccer balls and cookies frosted like tennis balls. Serve punch or soft drinks.

• • • ■ ● ● ● ● ● ● ● ● ● ● ■ ● ● ● ● ● ● ●

PARTY 17
Word Spectacular

GEARED FOR: ADULTS

Prizes (pick one or two kinds, or have a variety set out for winners to choose from): crossword puzzle books, fancy pencils, erasable pens

Do ahead:
■ Read "What Makes a Great Party?" on pages ix–xi.
■ Select activities, prepare materials, and plan refreshments.

Welcome Table and Opening Activity
Supplies needed:
■ nametags decorated with letters
■ markers
■ paper, one piece per person
■ pencils, one per person
■ list of people to find

Hand out paper and pencils, show the list of people to find, then send guest on their searches for someone:
1. with a Z in his or her name
2. with a last name that could also be a first name
3. without a middle name
4. with *Anne* or *Andrew* for a middle name

5. with a name of a U. S. president

6. with a name beginning with G

7. with a three-letter name

8. with the name of a fictional character

Game: Round Robin Table Games

Supplies needed:

■ word games such as Scrabble, UpWords, and Boggle

■ pencils and paper for score keeping

Lay out table games for guests to choose from. Those who prefer not to play can keep score. Let the table games go on for about 30–45 minutes.

Game: Spelling Fun

Supplies needed:

■ index cards with one alphabet letter and its point value written on each card (one set per team)

■ poster board with eight 3x5-inch rectangles drawn across it (one per team)

(Point Values: a=1; b=4; c=3; d=4; e=1; f=4; g=4; h=2; i=2; j=4; k=4; l=3; m=3; n=2; o=1; p=4; q=4; r=2; s=3; t=3; u=3; v=4; w=4; x=4; y=4; z=4)

Divide into teams. Give each team a set of index cards to distribute within their group. The leader calls out a word that is eight letters or less and has no duplicate letters. One at a time, team members with letters for the word places them on the poster board grid to spell out the word. If a letter is placed in the wrong box, teammates may ask for it to be repositioned. The first team to spell out the word correctly wins the added values of the letters.

(Suggested words: cabin; party; author; action; zero; quick; extra; diploma; famous; quagmire; howdy; justice; vibrate; flax; prince; jumped; orange; rickshaw; melon; gloves; bowtie; purchase; mustard; abode; boxes; bunch; zebra; yarn; lazy; quail; garden; and qualms.)

Bible Emphasis
Sing songs such as "O Word of God Incarnate" and "Wonderful Words of Life." Read Psalm 119:105 and John 1:1-3, 14. Discuss the power of words to harm or help. Invite people share positive stories in which words were used to celebrate, heal, honor, or encourage. Mention that hiding God's Word in out hearts can help us use our own words in loving ways.

Refreshments
Serve cakes or cupcakes sprinkled with alphabet cereal or candy letters and cookies or gelatine treats cut with alphabet cookie cutters and coffee, tea, and punch or lemonade.

Art Party

GEARED FOR: ADULTS

Prizes for this party could include: candy, drawing pencils, small sketch pads, masterpiece postcards, or stationery

Do ahead:
■ Read "What Makes a Great Party?" on pages ix–xi.
■ Select activities, prepare materials, and plan refreshments.

Welcome Table and Opening Activity
Supplies needed:
■ nametags
■ markers
■ paintings (by a local artist and reproductions/prints by well-known artists, such as Norman Rockwell, Monet, Grandma Moses, and Andrew Wyeth)
■ paper, one piece per person
■ pencils, one per person

Place prints or paintings around the room and number them. As guests arrive, give them paper and pencils, and ask them to identify each picture by the artist. Give the answers before beginning the next part of the program.

Game: Draw to Win
Supplies needed:
- blank paper
- markers

Divide the group into teams of eight or ten to compete against each other in drawing. The leader whispers the name of an object to the representative of each team, who races back to the team and begins drawing silently. When one team guesses the object correctly, change representatives and continue for about ten drawings. The team that guesses the most pictures correctly wins and members receive a prize.

Game: Curlique
Supplies needed:
- paper with curly scribble on it, one per person (all the same)
- drawing pencil or dark marker, one per person

Give each person a paper with the same curly scribble on it. Each player creates a drawing that includes the scribble, then names and signs his or her artwork. Allow five minutes to draw, and then have each person display his or her creation. Reward every artist with applause and a piece of candy.

Game: Art Foolishness
Supplies needed:
- piece of drawing paper, one per person
- sharp pencil, one per person

- watercolor paints and brushes for group to share
- colored pencils for group to share

Each guest sketches the outline of a picture, and then drawings are passed around so that each person gets someone else's. Everyone colors in the picture he or she received and returns the picture to the original artist.

Game: Name That Artist
- list of first names
- list of last names

Divide guests into two groups. Give one group the list of first names and the other, the list of last names. Group one shouts out a last name and group two reviews its list and guesses the appropriate first name. Continue with teams taking turns starting. (Answers: 1-e, 2-d, 3-f, 4-a, 5-c, 6-g, 7-h, 8-b, 9-i, 10-n, 11-m, 12-k, 13-j, 14-l, 15-o)

FIRST NAMES:	LAST NAMES:
1. Leonardo	a. Picasso
2. Andrew	b. Kincade
3. Claude	c. Rockwell
4. Pablo	d. Wyeth
5. Norman	e. da Vinci
6. Grandma	f. Monet
7. Michelangelo	g. Moses
8. Thomas	h. Buonarroti
9. Paul	i. Klee
10. Paul	j. Cassatt
11. René	k. de Goya
12. Francisco	l. Greenaway
13. Mary	m. Magritte
14. Kate	n. Cezanne
15. Georgia	o. O'Keeffe

Game: Art Quiz

Supplies needed:
- three bells for contestants to ring (if done as a quiz show)
- paper and pencils, one per person (if done as a group)

There are two ways to play this game and the person who gets the most questions right wins a prize.

A quiz show: Select three contestants to stand up front, ring a bell, and respond to the questions.

OR

Individual quizzes: Give everyone a piece of paper and a pencil to respond to the questions.

Questions:

1. Mix blue and red and what is the result? (purple)

2. Name three media used by portrait artists. (watercolor, pen and ink, oils, pastels, acrylic)

3. Mix blue and yellow and what is the result? (green)

4. Name three tools a painter needs. (easel, brush, paint, palette, spreading knife, canvas)

5. Mix yellow and red and what color is the result? (orange)

6. Of the four subjects most often painted, name two. (portraits, oceans, flowers, mountains)

7. Mix black and white and what color do you get? (gray)

8. Name a famous cartoonist. (Charles Shultz, Thomas Nast, or others)

9. When you add black to a color, do you get a shade or a tint? (a shade)

10. What did the cartoonist of "Calvin and Hobbes," Bill Waterson, retire to do? ("paint serious pictures")

Bible Emphasis

Have an artist or art lover lead this devotion, if possible. Bring in books of religious art or have guests share their favorite pieces. For example, Warner Sallman's "Christ at the Door" could be coupled with a reading of Revelation 3:20. Talk together about how art can both express our faith and communicate God's love.

Refreshments

Serve a large sheet cake, depicting a paintbrush or an artist's palette in the frosting. Or serve vanilla ice cream spread out on plates (a blank canvas) and have guests "paint" it with different toppings. Decorate the table with a bouquet of paintbrushes surrounded by little paint jars. Have several clear glass pitchers with various colors of punch.

PARTY 19

Floral Gala

GEARED FOR: WOMEN'S GROUP

Prizes for this party could include: silk flowers, flower magnets, small plants, flower-shaped candies, flower-design stickers, or flower-design note cards

Do Ahead:
■ Read "What Makes a Great Party?" on pages ix–xi.
■ Select activities, prepare materials, and plan refreshments.
■ Find and invite a knowledgeable gardener or ask each guest to bring a gardening tip to share.

■ Find a person with experience arranging flowers to lead the "Bouquets of Cheer" activity.

■ Notify guests of items they need to bring and have extras on-hand for those who forget.

■ Arrange for a soloist for the Bible emphasis.

Welcome Table and Opening Activity
Supplies needed:
■ nametags
■ markers
■ 15 magazine or calendar flower (or plant) close-ups, pasted on construction paper and numbered
■ one piece of paper per person
■ pencils, one per person

Display flower pictures around the room. Give everyone paper and a pencil and ask them to number the paper 1 through 15. Guests review the pictures and write the name of each flower beside the corresponding number. Review the answers. Those with the most correct identifications get a prize.

Game: Spelling Bee
Supplies needed:
■ paper and pencil for scorekeeping

Divide the group into two teams. Each team will be asked to send a contestant to the front to spell the name of a flower. If team one contestant can't spell it correctly, the person from team two can try. Give 100 points for each correct spelling. The winning team members get prizes. (Suggested words: poinsettia, columbine, hyacinth, lupine, goldenrod, pansy, and impatiens).

Activity: Garden Swap

Supplies needed:

- a set of numbers, beginning at 1 and going as high as there are participants
- bowl with numbered slips of paper
- "swappable" gardening items from guests
- extra "swappables" for those who forget

Each guest should bring to the party a small plant or new or gently used gardening item to swap. Be clear on a price range for those who opt to purchase something new. Items should be brought gift-wrapped or in pretty bags.

Gather in a circle and place all the "swappables" in the center. Pass around a bowl with slips of paper numbered according to the number of guests. Number 1 chooses and opens an item. Number 2 may take number 1's gift or open a new one from the center. If a person loses her gift, she may take another opened item or take a new one from the center. A gift may be passed around only three times during a round. The game is over when everyone has a gift.

Game: Flower Guess and Gardening Tips

Supplies needed:

- large sheets of newsprint paper
- colored pencils or markers
- special guest/expert in horticulture

Divide guests into two or more teams. Give each team colored pencils or markers and paper. Have each team send up a representative to the host, who will name a flower to draw for their groups. The first group to guess the flower correctly wins a point, and another "artist" takes over. The team with the most points wins prizes. Do about 10 rounds. (Suggested flowers: rose, violet, hibiscus, pansy, morning glory, tulip, petunia, marigold, poppy, daffodil, lily, black-eyed Susan, daisy, bleeding hearts, sunflower, African violets, and orchid.) Have the guest gardner offer tips on gardening, especially about flowers the group drew. Alternatively, ask guests to share special hints with one another.

Activity: Bouquets of Cheer
Supplies needed:
- silk flowers and foliage (brought by guests or party committee)
- floral foam
- knives, to cut foam to size
- baskets and vases (resale shops are a good source for these)
- wire cutters

Have a flower arranger give tips and invite guests to arrange the flowers. (Deliver arrangements to homebound friends later.)

Bible Emphasis
Have a soloist sing a garden-related hymn, such as "Rose of Sharon" or "I Come to the Garden." Read Bible texts with plants and flowers, such as Flowering Pomegranate (Numbers 13:23), Saffron (Song of Solomon 4:14), Flax (Joshua 2:6); and Rose of Sharon, and the Lily of the Valley (Song of Solomon 2:1 and Hosea 14:4). Invite guests to share how nature reveals God to them.

Refreshments
Use napkins with flowers or plants and serve vegetables and edible flowers with dip, and cakes decorated with flowers along with punch and/or tea and coffee.

PARTY 20

Not Your Usual Auction

GEARED FOR: ADULTS

Do ahead:

■ Read "What Makes a Great Party?" on pages ix–xi.

■ Review activities, prepare materials, and plan refreshments.

■ Gather sufficient "currency" for the auction. Possibilities for currency include paper, dried beans, toothpicks, craft sticks, and buttons.

■ Prepare bowls according to Opening Activity.

■ Notify guests in publicity to bring unwrapped "white elephants" (humorous giveaways) in good condition.

■ Gather extra white elephants for those who forget.

■ Secure a primary auctioneer and a relief auctioneer.

Welcome Table and Opening Activity

Supplies needed:

■ nametags

■ markers

■ 20 plastic bowls prepared according to bowl instructions

■ resealable sandwich bags, one per guest

Bowl instructions—fill with selected currency and label bowls as follows (modify instructions to suit your group):

1. If you aren't wearing a watch, give 2 to "purchase" the time from someone wearing a watch.

2. If you are wearing some black clothing, take 2.

3. If you are right-handed, take 2.

4. If you are left-handed, take 3.

5. If you arrived early, take 3.

6. If you buckled someone into a car seat today, take 5.

7. If you skipped breakfast today, put 3 into the bowl.

8. If you are wearing shoes with Velcro, take 2.

9. If you prayed today, take 5.

10. If you have brown eyes, take 2. If you don't, give 2 from your own bag to someone with brown eyes.

11. If you have a fifty-cent piece in your pocket, take 3.

12. If you read the Bible today, take 2.

13. If you ate an apple today, take 3.

14. If you play an instrument, take 2.

15. If you washed dishes today, take 3.

16. If you like to ski, take 2.

17. If you are wearing a sweater, take 4.

18. If you have a state quarter with you, take 3.

19. If you are wearing rings on more than one finger, take 2.

20. If you wear eyeglasses, take 4.

Pass out sandwich bags and explain that to gather currency for the auction, they need to visit the bowls that are placed around the room and follow the printed instructions. Send guests on their quest for currency and when all have finished, gather together for the auction.

Activity: Not Your Usual Auction

Supplies needed:

- public address system for auctioneer (optional)
- numbered paper plates for bidding, one per person
- extra white elephants
- bags for carrying purchases home

Place all the white elephants on a table. Pass out the numbered bidding. Explain: *"We're going to have an auction using the currency you gathered. When you want to bid on something, hold up your bidding number. I'll acknowledge you by number."*

A good auctioneer can keep the interest growing by finding an item's unique selling point, whether real or humorous. For example, *""What will you bid for these vintage black rubber boots? Imagine them planted with flowers in your garden!"* The auctioneer should get as high a bid as possible and then quickly move to the next item. Continue the auction until all of the items are sold or all currency spent. When the auctioneer gets tired, have the relief auctioneer step in for a little while.

Bible Emphasis

Read the poem "The Touch of the Master's Hand," then sing together "Since Jesus Came into My Heart."

"The Touch of the Master's Hand" by Myra Brooks Welch

'Twas battered and scarred, and the auctioneer
Thought it scarcely worth his while
To waste much time on the old violin,
But he held it up with a smile:

"What am I bidden, good folks," he cried,
"Who'll start the bidding for me?"
"A dollar, a dollar"; then, "Two!" "Only two?
Two dollars, and who'll make it three?

"Three dollars, once; three dollars, twice;
Going for three—" But no,
From the room, far back, a gray-haired man
Came forward and picked up the bow;

Then, wiping the dust from the old violin,
And tightening the loose strings,
He played a melody pure and sweet
As a caroling angel sings.

The music ceased, and the auctioneer,
With a voice that was quiet and low,
Said: "What am I bid for the old violin?"
And he held it up with the bow.

"A thousand dollars, and who'll make it two?
Two thousand! And who'll make it three?
Three thousand, once, three thousand, twice,
And going, and gone," said he.

The people cheered, but some of them cried,
"We don't quite understand
What changed its worth." Swift came the reply:
"The touch of the master's hand."

ask this

And many a man with life out of tune,
And battered and scarred with sin,
Is auctioned cheap to the thoughtless crowd,
Much like the old violin.

A "mess of pottage," a glass of wine;
A game—and he travels on.
He is "going" once, and "going" twice,
He's "going" and almost "gone."

But the Master comes, and the foolish crowd
Never can quite understand
The worth of a soul and the change that's
wrought
By the touch of the Master's hand.

Refreshments

Serve finger snacks that people can eat during the auction, such as
cheese and crackers and vegetables and dip, and end the evening
with cake, coffee, tea, and punch.

PARTY 21

Track and Field Day

GEARED FOR: ANY AGE GROUP

Prizes for this party could include gold, silver, and bronze awards. These can easily be made by cutting and covering or painting 3-inch circles, or by using purchased medallion stickers and attaching a ribbon.

Do ahead:
■ Read "What Makes a Great Party?" on pages ix–xi.
■ Select activities, prepare materials, and plan refreshments.

Welcome Table and Opening Activity
Do ahead:
■ Set out pitchers of ice water and cups.
■ Find volunteers to offer exercise demonstrations.
Supplies needed:
■ nametags
■ markers

Offer demonstrations of simple exercises by several enthusiasts. After a few minutes, ask any guests who want to, to join in.

Warm-up Activity: Relay Races
Do ahead:
■ Mark start and finish lines with chalk or masking tape.

Divide the group into teams of six or eight. Have them line up and complete several relay races walking, skipping, hopping, and walking backwards. Give medals to the winning teams for each relay.

Main Activity: Olympic Competitions
Note: People can sign up for as many as four different competitions. Those guests who aren't participating in a race can become the cheering audience.
Do ahead:
■ Mark courses with masking tape or chalk.
■ Select timekeepers.
Supplies needed:
■ stop watches
■ sturdy foam dinner plates or sponge flying disc
■ yardstick and tape measure
■ paper and pens for keeping score
■ sponge ball
■ masking tape
■ heavy cardboard gift wrap tube, wrapped in newspaper and packing tape for added strength and weight
■ newsprint or poster boards

▲ *Cross Country Race:* This event consists of "race walking" around a route marked with tape or chalk throughout different rooms and corridors of the area. When all contestants finish, award first-, second-, and third-place prizes.

▲ *Discus Throw*: Participants stand behind a line and throw, discus-style, a round foam dinner plate or a sponge flying disc. Let each contestant have two tries. The three with the longest throws receive appropriate prizes. If space is limited, instead of going for the longest actual throw, ask contestants to hit a sign with a distance, such as 80 meters, 100 meters, or "Out of the Stadium," indicated on it.

▲ *High Jump*: Experiment to see what height is a good average height to start with for your group. Each contestant jumps over a yardstick with a short run. When everyone has tried, raise the stick five inches and let them try again. Keep going up until only one person can jump over it. Give medals to the top three participants.

▲ *Shot Put*: Contestants gather at a starting line. One at a time, they throw a sponge ball Shot-Put-style. Mark the landing spots with the contestant's name on masking tape until all have tried. Give out prizes to the longest distances.

▲ *500-Inch Dash:* Measure out 500 inches. Time contestants as they run, one at a time. Winners receive appropriate medals.

▲ *Javelin Throw:* Mark a line. Each contestant throws the cardboard tube javelin from behind the line. Have two or more judges mark where the javelin lands with masking tape and the contestant's name. Award appropriate prizes.

Bible Emphasis
Have someone share a short devotional on 2 Timothy 4:7, focusing on the need to stay the course in the Christian life.

Refreshments
Serve healthy finger foods, such as raw veggies and granola bars. Also offer cookies, sports drinks, punch, coffee, and tea.

SECTION FOUR

Outreach Parties

Perhaps the best way to reach outsiders is via an informal gathering for the express purpose of interesting them in the church and its message. A pleasurable evening could make all the difference in someone's spiritual journey. Active church members should do their best to invite non-churchgoers, former churchgoers, neighbors, and friends. At the party, each active member needs to think of himself or herself as a host of the party and work to welcome and get to know the visitors. Don't make the mistake of putting great effort into planning a wonderful party, then neglect visitors.

As always, pre-planning is very important. Be sure that the work is not left to a few. Involve a committee of people who will work, plan, pray, and will invite others. Collect all necessary items and have them within reach. Be sure publicity is done early and give advance notice to the person handling the Bible Emphasis.

At each party announce the next program along with the date and time. In church, announce it three weeks in advance. Have it listed on the church calendar. Put several posters around the church and put similar information on post cards and mail them about two weeks ahead of time to regulars and possible guests.

The Bible equates a cheerful heart with good medicine (Proverbs 17:22). Therefore, include all who come in the joys and pleasures of a Christ-centered party. And do everything possible to make the Outreach Parties exactly that: parties that really reach out beyond your church roster.

PARTY 22
First Time Fun Time

Prizes for this party could include: a variety of candies in a basket, small memo pads, small magnets

Do ahead:
- Read "What Makes a Great Party?" on pages ix–xi.
- Select activities, prepare materials, and plan refreshments.

Welcome Table and Opening Activity
Supplies needed:
- nametags
- markers

■ one piece of paper per guest
■ pencils, one per guest
■ list of people to find printed on newsprint. Have greeters at the table to ensure that sure all guests get a nametag and a warm greeting.

Have new people join with the friend(s) they came with (or pair them with outgoing persons). Post the following list and send guests to gather the signature of a person who:

1. Was born in this month
2. Lived in Boston
3. Is wearing black clothing
4. Has more than three pets
5. Teaches school
6. Is left-handed
7. Likes sports
8. Doesn't like to sing
9. Likes mushrooms

10. Has served overseas (as a missionary, in the military, or in the Peace Corps)

Activity: Storytelling
Supplies needed:
■ bell, one per group
■ tape recorder and tape (optional)

Seat guests in circles, ten to a circle and appoint a leader within each group. The leader starts a story with a simple phrase, such as: "Once upon a time, there was a church event." Then the person on his or her left adds to the story, trying to include some details about people from the opening activity, for instance, "Then the phone began to ring and JoJo picked it up with her left hand." The leader rings the bell and the next person continues the story with other details about guests. The details are woven into a story, however far-fetched. The game leader keeps the story moving by ringing the bell and can create a cliffhanger by stopping someone mid-sentence. Consider recording the whole story to play back during refreshments.

Game: Drop the Blanket
Supplies needed:
■ blanket, one per group

Divide the guests into groups of twenty. Divide each group into two teams. Give each group a blanket. To play the game, both teams introduce themselves to each other. Then one team holds up a blanket by two ends. One team member stands behind the blanket. The other team is on the other side of the blanket and cannot see the person hidden by the blanket. The other team says, "Drop the blanket!" When the blanket drops, they have until the blanket hits the floor to shout out the person's name. If the team guessed right, they get a point. Then it is the other team's turn to guess. The first team with ten points wins.

Game: Stand or Sit
Everyone sits in a circle with a leader in the center. Guests remain standing until a command has them sit, then rise and sit as commands require.
Suggested Commands:
1. Everyone who is right-handed, stand up.
2. Everyone with a dime in his or her pocket, sit down.
3. Everyone born in October, stand up.

4. Everyone with tie shoes, sit down.

5. Everyone wearing green, stand up.

6. Everyone with a digital watch sit down.

7. Everyone who ate ice cream today, stand up.

8. Everyone who lives within one mile, sit down.

9. Everyone who drives a GM car, stand up.

10. Everyone who has black hair, sit down.

11. Everyone wearing a sweater, stand up.

12. Everyone who wrote an e-mail today, sit down.

13. Those standing shake hands with those sitting.

Activity: Match Up

Supplies needed:

▪ criteria listed on poster board (modify to suit your group):

     o born in the same month

     o drives the same make and model car

     o born in the same decade

     o wearing the same color clothing

     o lives in the same zip code

     o shares a similar occupation

Point out the criteria list and explain that everyone searches for two partners who meet one of the criteria. Allow a few minutes for guests to talk about other things that they have in common. Encourage new friends to sit together for the Bible emphasis.

Bible Emphasis

Recruit a personable Bible teacher to share some thoughts on how God knows us and cares about each one of us. Two possible texts are Psalm 139:14-16 and Jeremiah 1:5. The devotional should be kept short (five minutes) and be positive in tone. End with prayer and an invitation to return to a coming activity and/or church services (without being pushy).

Refreshments

If you recorded your storytelling game, play the tape during refreshment time.

Serve sandwich halves, fruit and vegetable platters, cookies, punch, coffee, and tea. Make sure active church members are talking with—but not pressuring—visitors. Have several people at the door to bid the guests goodbye. Thank visitors for coming and assure them how much you'd like to see them again.

PARTY 23
Hobby Share

GEARED FOR: OUTREACH TO ADULTS

Do ahead:

■ Read "What Makes a Great Party?" on pages ix–xi.

■ At least two weeks before the party, find people who are willing to share a hobby, collection, or talent (music, dance, comedy, dramatic reading). Include church members, friends, and people from the community.

■ Secure volunteers for the Bible emphasis and give them sufficient notice to practice.

Activity: Viewing Displays

■ Prepare a list of all those who will display hobbies or collections. Use this list to create promotional fliers and posters.

■ Set up plenty of tables for displays.

Enlist volunteers to help set up and watch displays while hobbyists are not present. Devote the first half of the event to viewing the displays.

Activity: Entertainment

Do ahead:

■ Plan the schedule of about 10 performers from the church group or friends of the church.

■ Prepare programs listing the entertainers.

■ Secure an emcee.

■ Set up an area with a stage, sound system, and chairs.

Culminate the evening with a stage show of performances, hosted by an emcee. Be sure that each presenter is given attention and is applauded. End with a round of applause for all performers.

Bible Emphasis

Invite a team to present the devotional in an artistic manner. For example, an artist can draw a picture while a reader reads a familiar passage, such as Psalm 23; a dancer can join movement to an instrumental version of a favorite hymn, such as "How Great Thou Art," or a team can do a skit of one of Jesus' parables.

Refreshments

Make drinks available throughout the event, but save full refreshments to the end of the party. Simple fare should suffice, such as a variety of cookies with coffee, tea, and punch. Or consider having people whose hobby is baking prepare refreshments. Label each baked good with the baker's name and perhaps even with the recipes. During refreshments, be sure the church people intersperse with the visitors so that all guests will feel comfortable.

PARTY 24
For a Good Cause Carnival (Fundraiser)

GEARED FOR: ADULTS AND OLDER CHILDREN

Prizes for this party could include fun-size candy in baskets and pails.

Do ahead:
■ Read "What Makes a Great Party?" on pages ix–xi.
■ Prepare materials and plan refreshments.
■ Borrow and/or rent carnival games from a local business, ministry, school, or individuals.

■ Secure game hosts.

■ Request that church members donate white elephant (funny give away) items for the Silent Auction.

■ Select the cause for which you will raise funds. To make this truly an outreach event, choose a community-based organization local cause, or a church outreach such as a clinic or day care.

■ Make sure that everyone invited knows this is a fundraiser and fully describe the cause funds will support.

■ Create pass slips for any children who attend.

Welcome Table and Opening Activity

Do ahead:

■ Make "The Price of Humor" poster for cost of jokes (see sample below)

■ Print "Virtual Pledge" on a 3 x 5 index card for each guest.

■ Glue jokes and anecdotes from old magazines to pieces of colored construction paper (at least one per expected guest) and hide them around the room.

Supplies needed:

■ nametags

■ markers

■ pencil, one per person

■ posters illustrating the cause for which the funds are being raised

■ pennies for children

Gather guests together and describe the cause for which you are raising funds. Hand out

"Virtual Pledge" cards and pencils, and explain that throughout the evening they will be making virtual pledges, ranging from ten cents to a dollar each and that at the end of the evening, pledges will be totaled to guide their donations. Hand out a specific number of free pass slips to children, so they won't feel left out or concerned about not having any money.

Invite guests to search for the jokes that are hidden in the room. Once everyone has found a joke, review the "Price of Humor" poster and invite guests to "purchase" a hearing of each others' jokes. The cost of hearing each joke is listed on the buyer's "Virtual Pledge" card.

Activities: Games and Laughter

The following three events can take place simultaneously and will allow people to participate in activities according to their abilities and interests.

▲ *Carnival games:* Set up games such as bean-bag-toss, squirting targets, numbered ducks floating in a tub, clothespin in the milk bottle, and guess the number of marbles in a jar. Consider renting games such as a dunk tank or moon jump. Carnival games can be going on throughout the event while other activities are taking place. Post a virtual pledge fee for each game and have players add that amount to their "Virtual Pledge" cards. Distribute candy as prizes.

▲ *Story share:* For a less strenuous activity, host a storytelling time. Most people have amusing stories of getting ready for Sunday church or attending a wedding. A game host starts things off and each story told requires a pledge of 10¢. Participants come and go as they please.

▲ *Make Me Laugh If You Can*: Contestants earn candy prizes by withstanding the efforts of the game host to make them laugh. The contestant sits while the game-host acts foolish, trying to get the person to laugh. If the person does laugh, he or she is assessed a 10¢ pledge. If the person stays solemn, the game host doles out candy. To make this game more fun, laughers can be assessed a forfeit as well as a pledge. Suggested forfeits include: sing part of an opera, gospel, or folk song, laugh out loud for one minute, quote a nursery rhyme, or touch your toes.

Activity: White Elephant Silent Auction
Supplies needed:
■ donated white elephants displayed on a long table
■ bidding sheets for each item with space for bidders to record their names and bids—type on the bottom of sheet: "This bid is for *real* money. Bidder must pay to take home the item at the end of the event." Consider assigning a comically low minimum bid to each object.

The auction and Photo Op can take place at the same time. Announce the start of these two events and draw the games to a close. Explain that the auction bids are real—closing bids will be collected at the end and players will take home the items. If someone wants to bid on an item, he or she signs the bid sheet accompanying that item and posts a bid amount. Other people can come along and outbid each other, so encourage people to pass the table more than once.

Activity: Photo Op
Supplies needed:
- digital cameras, photo printer, and photo paper
- dress-up clothes on hangers for adults and children
- a sign announcing that the photographer is open for business
- portable coat rack
- table for displaying photos
- an experienced photographer
- an experienced photo printer

For this activity, you need to create an elegant place to take photographs—perhaps a garden bench with a trellis and silk garlands. Nearby hang adult and children's dress-up clothes on a portable coat rack. Try to include a variety of styles: nice vintage, odd, big, and vibrant-colored clothes and accessories.

You may want to set a minimum pledge amount for each photo. Have the photographer take the pictures and then pass that camera along to the photo printer to print. Ask the guests to wait for the pictures to be developed and, if the photo is acceptable, add the pledge amount to their "Virtual Pledge" cards.

Closing and Bible Emphasis
- envelopes
- information on the cause being supported
- results of Silent Auction

Announce the results of the Silent Auction and have purchasers come by the auction table after the close of the evening to settle up. Note that anyone who has had a change of heart (or purse) can opt out of the purchase by notifying the host of the auction table and the item will be offered to the next highest bidder.

Someone representing the cause could share words of thanks with the guests. Have guests total pledges on their "Virtual Pledge" cards and make their donations by putting them in an envelope and giving them to a designated person. Read Luke 6:38, offer a prayer of dedication for the money raised and offer a sincere word of thanks giving to God for blessing both those who give and receive.

Refreshments
Serve classic carnival food such as popcorn, peanuts, candy apples, and soda or lemonade. It is best not to charge a fee or pledge for refreshments, although guests will often make a donation if a basket is available.

This Old Thing?
(An Antique I.D. Party)

GEARED FOR: OUTREACH TO ADULTS OR FAMILIES

Prizes for this party could include old-fashioned candies.

Do ahead:
■ Read "What Makes a Great Party?" on pages ix–xi.
■ Prepare materials and plan refreshments.
■ Find volunteer *unofficial* appraisers from among antique experts and enthusiasts.
■ Stress in the publicity that appraisals are unofficial and not valid for sales or insurance purposes.

Welcome Table and Opening Activity

Supplies needed:
■ nametags
■ markers
■ "bakery ticket" numbers for each person bringing items
■ obscure objects from the past
■ one piece of paper per person
■ pencils, one for each person

Number and display obscure object from the past. Hand out paper and pencils and ask guests as they arrive if they have antiques to show. Give "bakery tickets" to those who do and explain that numbers will be announced, so it is fine to participate in the other activities.

Have arriving guests review the objects on display, write down numbers and guesses about the identity and use of each object. When all are done, review the objects and their uses and give those guests with the most correct answers a prize.

Main Program: Antique Identifications

Supplies needed:

- chairs
- public address system
- two or more unofficial antique appraisers

Set up chairs in rows like a typical audience. Place a long table for the appraisers at the front of the area. Set up the microphone in front of the table. Have space along the side for the next five people to wait their turns. If you have two or more appraisers, one or two can be assessing an artifact while one is announcing his or her findings to the public using the microphone. As appraisals are completed, announce the next set of "bakery numbers" so people come to the appraisal area.

Side Show: Then and Now Display

Supplies needed:

- old items and their contemporary counterparts, such as:
- rollerskates/rollerblades
- typewriter/computer
- crank/rotary/cordless/cell phones

- wax cylinder/record album/CD
- reel-to-reel tape recorder/cassette tape recorder/ digital tape recorder
- knife/electric food chopper

Display older items beside their modern counterparts and invite guests to peruse the display.

Side Show: Antiques at Work

Supplies needed:
- antiques and skilled users to demonstrate them
- reproductions

Invite people to bring and demonstrate antique tools. Also have on-hand some reproductions that guests can touch.

Suggested demonstrations:
- spinning with a wheel and a drop spindle
- writing with a quill pen
- whittling
- making rope with a plying machine
- making lace
- churning butter
- carding wool
- drinking with a "common dipper"

Bible Emphasis

Explain: *"Second Chronicles records a wonderful discovery of an heirloom,"* and have a good storyteller retell 2 Chronicles 34 (the

story of the discovery of the Book of the Law in the Temple during King Josiah's reign). Talk about the timeless treasure we have in the gospel of Jesus.

Refreshments
To make sure that no antiques are harmed, have refreshments last, after the displays are covered or removed. Serve ice cream sundaes with old-fashioned toppings with ice water or lemonade.

PARTY 26
"Thank You" Party

GEARED FOR: ADULTS

Do ahead:
- Read "What Makes a Great Party?" on pages ix–xi.
- Prepare materials and plan refreshments.
- Plan the guest list to fit the occasion, including family, and possibly friends, of those honored or even the whole congregation.
- Send special invitations to those who are being thanked and their guests. This party can reach into the community.
- Give general announcements to other guests, using a telephone crew for reminders.

■ Secure a Master of Ceremonies.

■ Decide on catering or potluck.

■ For catering, it is necessary to have reservations well ahead of time.

■ For potluck, you'll need to know how much food to plan for and have a sign-up list for food well in advance.

■ Ask several people to be ready to describe a special event that shows the blessing the honored guests have been to the church.

The "Thank You" Party can be adapted to recognize anyone within the church fellowship. You might want to celebrate the Christian education workers, those who have achieved a milestone of service, church officers, staff, choir members, missionaries on home assignment, or an anniversary of your pastor's tenure. One such party a year could be enough, but a "thank you" is always in style. It should be a fun time and time of remembrance.

Welcome Table and Opening Activities
Supplies needed:

■ nametags
■ markers
■ paper and pencils for each person
■ newsprint, several pieces posted or on easels
■ colored markers

▲ *Investigation:* Hand each person a piece of paper that says, "Find two people you do not know and discover their names, their occupations, and their birthplaces." Have them start immediately. When most people have arrived, have guests form groups to share the information.

▲ *Creation of one liners:* As guests arrive, encourage them to write on newsprint words of praise, thanks, or blessing for the person or persons being honored.

Main Activity: Dinner

If it's financially feasible, have this party catered. If a fee for a catered meal is charged, those being honored and their guests should get complimentary tickets. If some guests cannot afford tickets, other guests might be willing to give extra to offset the costs of others. If the expense of catering is prohibitive, make the dinner a potluck. The dessert could be a cake with an inscription for the occasion or potluck desserts that are themed around the preferences of the person or persons being honored.

Program: Honoring the Special Guests

Appoint a Master of Ceremonies who can keep the program moving and praise the accomplishments of those being honored, mentioning each one by name, and (if possible) a specific accomplishment of each person. A media presentation of ministry highlights is always welcomed.

Choose program features from those listed or plan others that fit your honorees:

▲ *One Liners and Words of Thanks*: Ask everyone to share one of the words of praise, thanks, or blessing they wrote on the newsprint, identifying the person being honored. Save the newsprint to give to the honorees at the end of the party. Have guests who have prepared ahead of time share stories about the honorees and their importance to the church. Then open the sharing to anyone who wishes to add more accolades.

▲ *Saluting You*: Divide into groups to create "human sculptures" that represent the contributions of the honoree(s). Invite each group to present its sculpture while guests guess what it represents. Then give these groups ten minutes to create cheers or short poems saluting those being honored. Provide time for each group to present or lead others in their cheers.

▲ *Response*: Make sure honorees are apprised that they will be given a chance to respond. Some may choose to offer a simple thank you while others may want to share a story or devotional.

▲ *Other Possible Activities*: Depending on your church and the people being honored, one or more of the following activities might be appropriate:
■ a musical presentation by a choir or other church musical group
■ media presentations (video, Power Point, scrapbooks and photo albums)
■ a money or card tree, to which people clip dollar bills or greeting cards and notes

Bible Emphasis
Sing a few favorite songs of the guests being honored. Then have a speaker give a brief message on Philippians 1:3, stressing that Paul always thanked those who worked with him in the work of the Lord. After a closing prayer, have a reception line to thank all those who have been honored during the evening.

Date   Party Given   Comments

Date	Party Given	Comments

Date	Party Given	Comments

Date   Party Given   Comments

_____

_____

_____

_____

_____

_____

_____

_____

_____

_____

_____

_____

_____

_____

_____

_____

_____

Date   Party Given   Comments

_____

_____

_____

_____

_____

_____

_____

_____

_____

_____

_____

_____

_____

_____

_____

_____

Date	Party Given	Comments

CELEBRATE GOOD TIMES!

Date	Party Given	Comments

Date   Party Given   Comments